CW00672587

First In!
Parachute
Pathfinder Company

To the Memory of:

John Lander and 'Boy' Wilson
all those who lost their lives or limbs in the
service of the Company
and to all who served with it.

FIRST IN!
Parachute
Pathfinder Company

A History of the
21st Independent Parachute Company
the original pathfinders
of British Airborne Forces
1942 – 1946

England	France
Algeria	Holland
Tunisia	Greece
Sicily	Norway
Italy	Palestine

RON KENT

B.T. Batsford Ltd
London

Hippocrene Books
New York

First published 1979
Copyright Ron Kent 1979

Printed in Great Britain by
Redwood Burn Ltd.,
Trowbridge and Esher.
Phototypeset by Granada Graphics

for the Publishers B. T. Batsford Ltd,
4 Fitzhardinge Street, London W1H 0AH
and Hippocrene Books Inc,
171 Madison Avenue New York N.Y. 10016

ISBN 0 7134 2199 1

Contents

14 List of Illustrations

Maps

Acknowledgment
The Author and Publishers thank the Imperial War Museum for
their permission to reproduce illustrations 6, 7, 8, 9 and 10.

Foreword

The 21st Independent Parachute Company was a unique body of men founded in 1942 by Major John Lander TD, whose brain child it was.

Assisted by Captain B. A. Wilson MC and Lieutenant R. E. Spivey and with the blessing of Lieutenant General Frederick Browning, commander of the 1st British Airborne Division, John Lander started recruiting the 180 men which was to be the Company's normal war strength from very humble barracks in the peacetime garrison of Larkhill on Salisbury Plain.

The Company had a life span of only four years; from 1942 until 1946. In that short space of time members of the Company saw active service in Algeria, Tunisia, Sicily, Italy, the south of France, Holland, Norway, Greece and Palestine. A 'regular Cooks' tour' as one of them likes to describe it, although that venerable travel agency would hardly have recommended the mode of transport and the accommodation which the Company was obliged to adopt.

The Company was unique in that no other airborne forces (enemy or allied) had anything like it. The Germans, first in the field in the use of airborne forces, certainly had no equivalent to John Lander's pathfinders. Successful though the small-scale attacks of the Germans on selected targets in the Low Countries and Scandinavia were in May 1940, the large-scale airborne attack on Crete in May 1941 would have benefited by a pathfinder force such as John Lander had in mind.

Fresh from their recent successful operation in Greece which secured the Corinth Canal, German parachute and glider-borne troops descended on Crete on 20 May 1941 with the full support of the Luftwaffe. They sustained fearful casualties even before landing and although the campaign was successfully concluded in a mere ten days, Crete became 'the graveyard of German parachutists' according to their commander, General Kurt Student. Afterwards, Hitler told him 'The day of the paratrooper is over'. For the British, it was only beginning.

The success of German airborne operations in May 1940 so

impressed Winston Churchill that, on 22 June 1940, he instructed General Ismay, then head of the Military Wing of the War Cabinet Secretariat, to set in motion the formation of 'a corps of at least five thousand parachute troops'.

It took the British a considerable time to get this concept under way. Unlike the Germans, the British had made no preparations for the training of parachute troops though there was a nucleus of enthusiastic glider pilots (amateur weekend sportsmen) entirely unconnected with the Army. Many of these, John Lander among them, came to the fore when the word went out from the War Office that an airborne force was to be formed.

Still, in 1940 Britain was only slowly recovering from the loss of men, arms, ammunition and equipment in France and Belgium. There was a shortage of aircraft and a certain understandable reluctance on the part of the RAF to accord the infant Army Air Corp any sort of priority. The most it felt able to do was to make available a few obsolete Whitley bombers and a handful of experienced parachute instructors.

Nevertheless, a small force of British parachutists carried out an attack on an aqueduct in southern Italy on 10 February 1941. All who took part were either killed or captured.

Almost exactly one year later, 119 officers and men of 2nd Parachute Battalion carried out a highly successful raid on a German radar station on the Normandy coast at Bruneval. Led by Major (later Lt. Col., DSO,MC) J. D. Frost the force returned, 14 men fewer, but with radar expert, Flight Sergeant E. W. F. Cox and the vital piece of equipment they had been sent to secure. In both these operations aircraft went astray. This could have jeopardised the men who took part and the success of both operations.

Lessons were being learned from these early beginnings and from a study of the German operations of 1940 and 1941. Not least of these was the realisation that the success of really large-scale attacks, on the Crete model, would be considerably enhanced if a small body of men could be dropped with pin-point accuracy to secure and mark dropping zones (DZ) and landing zones (LZ) for gliders.

These forerunners would not have to be dropped so far in advance of the main body as to lose the element of surprise. This meant that once on the ground they would have to act swiftly and efficiently. The navigational aids they carried would have to be carefully worked out so as to be manageable and to give the maximum assistance to the massed formations of aircraft bearing their expensively trained parachute battalions and glider-borne troops, transport and guns. The object was to ensure the delivery of whole units of company, battalion and brigade strength accurately at appointed places and on time.

This was the function of the 21st Independent Parachute Company. How to do it was the task of Major Lander and the men he gathered about him in the autumn of 1942. To assist him he had Wing Commander P. May and his 38 Wing of the Royal Air Force and two complimentary pieces of ingenious equipment called 'Eureka' and 'Rebecca'. The function of 'Eureka' and 'Rebecca' is explained later.

This is the story of how John Lander set about his task; of the men he selected to carry it out and of their achievements both in their specific role as pathfinders and in their wider role as an independent company subject only to directions from the Brigade or Divisional commander to whom they might be assigned.

The History in Outline

July	Company installed in olive grove encampment near M'saken on Kairouan/Sousse road and is joined by Lieutenants Baker, D'Arifat and Grierson.
5	Divisional ammunition dump blows up.
9/10	Operation 'Husky' – the invasion of Sicily begins.
13/14	Operation 'Manston' – the 1st Parachute Brigade's operation against the Primosole Bridge, Catania Plain, Sicily – members of the Company in action. Major Lander killed over Sicily.
17/18	Airborne withdrawn from Sicily. Captain Wilson becomes CO and Lieutenant Spivey, 2nd in command.
25	Mussolini resigns and is arrested in Italy.
August 17	Sicily campaign successfully concluded.
31	Company parachute exercise in Tunisia.
September 3	Invasion of Italy at Reggio.
6	1st Airborne Division ordered to land (sea-borne) at Taranto.
8	Company at Bizerta and embarks on HMS Cruiser *Orion*.
9	Company lands at Taranto. HMS *Abdiel* mined in Taranto harbour and 6th (Welsh) Parachute Battalion sustains heavy casualties. Perimeter defence of Taranto. Platoon patrol first into Bari. Company's first casualty in Italy at Castellaneta. Divisional Commander, Major General Hopkinson killed in subsequent attack there. Major General Down CBE becomes Divisional commander.
13	Division based 20 miles from Taranto.
17	Company moves up to Goioa del Colle.

25	Under the guns near Canosa.
26	Company clears airfield at Foggia. Private McKnight missing believed killed.
27	Company enters Foggia. Presses on to San Severo.
29	Apricena. Lieutenant Grierson badly wounded and evacuated to Tripoli.
October	78th Division takes over. Company taken out of action. Marches back to Barletta.
November 16	Take-off from Goioa del Colle for night drop using American flown Dakotas.
30	Company shipped back from Taranto to Bizerta. Captain Baker appointed to command 1st Independent Parachute Platoon to remain with 2nd Parachute Brigade in Italy.
December 2	Company by rail to Blida in Algeria – a five-day journey in cattle trucks.
24	Company embarks at Algiers for UK.
1944 January	Bassingham, Lincolnshire – Company receives replacements. Lieutenants Ashmore, Eastwood and Speller join the Company as platoon commanders. CSM Stewart replaces CSM Keirnan who, with others, leaves for OCTU. 1st Independent Parachute Platoon in Sicily. Major-General Roy Urquhart – Divisional Commander
April 8	Brigade exercise in Rutland. Oakham – dawn Dakota drop.
21	Exercise 'Mush' near Cirencester. Company moves into barracks at Newark.

June 1	Elements of 1st Independent Parachute Platoon take part in Operation 'Hasty' in Italy.
6	D Day – 1st Airborne Division in reserve. 1st Independent Parachute Platoon moves to Paestum, south of Salerno.
11	Company is briefed for drop on Evrecy.
12	Operation cancelled. Further operations planned, briefed and cancelled. Frequent forty-eight hour leaves after cancellations.
August 9	Company exercise in Lincolnshire.
15	Operation 'Dragoon' – landing in the South of France. 1st Independent Parachute Platoon first to land. Private Morley killed.
17	1st Independent Parachute Platoon return to Rome area.
September 10	Company briefed for Operation 'Comet' – the Arnhem operation in miniature.
11	Operation cancelled. Company stand by.
16	Briefing for Operation 'Market'.
17	Company jump north of the Lower Rhine using Stirlings and mark all DZs and LZs for first lift of Operation 'Market'.
18	Company mark DZs and LZs for 2nd lift and supply drops.
19	No. 1 Platoon marks LZ for Polish gliderborne elements.
19/25	Defence of Oosterbeek perimeter.
25/26	Withdrawal across Lower Rhine to Nijmegen minus heavy casualties.
27/28	Company survivors move down 'the Corridor' to Louvain near Brussels.

29	Flown back to Saltby and thence to Newark barracks.
October 12	Operation 'Manna' – elements of 1st Independent Parachute Platoon and 'C' Company, 4th Parachute Battalion land at Megara, near Athens in high wind.
October to January	Reception and training of replacements at Newark. More promotional departures.

1945

January	1st Independent Parachute Platoon moved to Salonika with 5th (Scottish) Parachute Battalion. Returns to Rome by air. Recalled to Greece – by sea from Brindisi to Pireaus. Street fighting drive into Athens. Prolonged street fighting in Athens. Lieutenant 'Jock' Boyd killed. Sergeant Yates and Private Wolf each earn MMs.
February	1st Independent Parachute Platoon returns to Italy where five operations in support of 8th Army are planned and cancelled.
March	Company parachute exercise in Yorkshire using Dakotas.
May 9	VE Day – Company flies into Norway at Stavanger and Gardemoen near Oslo. General duties in Norway marshalling and movement of German troops. 1st Independent Parachute Platoon returns to UK and disbanded, some rejoin the Company.
August 14	Japan capitulates.
October	Company leaves Norway. Disembarkation leave. Embarks for Palestine and joins 6th Airborne Division there.
November 6	Landing at Haifa. Move to Sarafand and then to Qastina airfield.

Demonstration drop at Amman, Jordania.
Qastina airfield raided by terrorists and Halifax bombers destroyed.
Private Cook killed at Petah Tiqva.
CO leaves.
Major Spivey becomes CO and on CSM Stewart's departure for demobilisation Sergeant Kent becomes CSM.
Company moves to Latrun Police Fort.
Exercise in Dead Sea Valley and hills around Jericho.

1946

February 22   Company exercise using Halifax aircraft over the Gaza strip.

May 28   Probably the last Company parachute exercise from Dakotas.

June   CSM Felix Hunt takes over from CSM Kent leaving for demobilisation.

September   Company disbanded in Palestine.

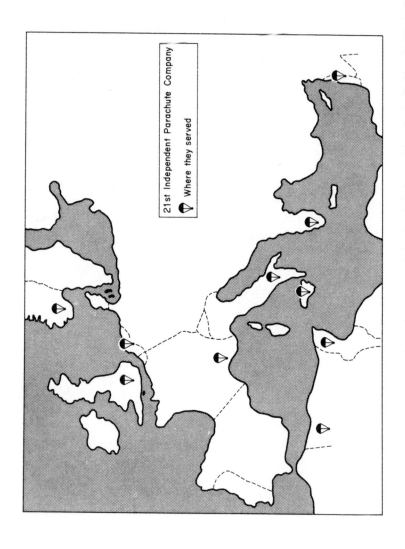

21st Independent Parachute Company

🪂 Where they served

1 LARKHILL
(and other places) – 1942

John Lander replaced the telephone receiver and spoke across the blanket covered table. 'That was Ringway. We have another 15 on their way to us. Will you lay on transport to meet them in Salisbury tomorrow afternoon? ETA 15.00 hours.' He was addressing his second in command, dapper, ex-cavalryman, Captain 'Boy' Wilson MC. The name 'Boy' had stuck with him since his days at Eton where he had been a contemporary of another 'Boy', Frederick 'Boy' Browning. Though Browning was now the General charged with the task of raising and training Britain's very first Airborne Division, he and Wilson were close friends. This friendship undoubtedly played its part in making the 21st Independent Parachute Company the unusual and exclusive formation which it became.

It was not so long since Captain Wilson himself had been a newcomer to the Company and Stan Brown and his close pal, Dick Wilkin had the task of initiating the new 2 I/C into the map-reading and orientation methods employed by the Company. On a totally dark night they sallied forth on Salisbury Plain and, setting a course on the map beforehand with the aid of a protractor, conducted the unknown Captain at a great rate on a jaunt from copse to ancient tumuli and other landmarks with the aid of a prismatic compass. They completed the course in record time and the much older Wilson, panting along in the rear, was completely convinced of the younger men's ability to navigate their way across country by night.

The 15 expected arrivals were the survivors of what, for them, were twenty-four very testing days.

Less than a month before they had been sent with five others, first to the depot of the Parachute Regiment at Hardwick Hall near Chester and then to the parachute training school at Ringway.

Though pre-selected by Major Lander they nevertheless had to pass the rigorous standards set by the regimental staff at the Depot. Any who failed to measure up to those standards were RTU'd ('returned to unit') within twenty-four hours.

Discipline at the Depot was under the strict and exacting eye of that awesome veteran of the Bruneval Raid, RSM 'Gerry' Strachan (ex- Black Watch), a very tough customer indeed. At Bruneval he had received three German bullets in the stomach. As one potential member of the Company observed: 'It is amazing that it is possible to admire a man and at the same time, loathe his guts.' Although no longer fit for active service, Gerry Strachan still performed a useful and necessary function at the Depot. Unlovable he might be, but he certainly merited the awe and respect of the young men who passed through his hands at Hardwick.

From reveille at 06.00 hours until 18.00 hours every day (save Sundays), and from that same early hour until 13.00 hours on Saturdays, the relentless programme proceeded, designed to weed out the men likely to be unsuited for full service as a parachutist. The programme was not only designed for this. Much of it was instructive and toughening, so that when the specific act of parachuting came, the nerves, the mind and the body, would be prepared for it. Prepared not only for that novel, exhilarating and, sometimes, shattering, experience but also for the exertion and tasks which were to follow. For parachuting was only another means of getting into action, like marching or being sea-landed.

A forced march of ten miles in two hours in full battle kit; a battle course over a bewildering series of obstacles, crawling in mud under close machine-gun fire; psychological tests applied immediately after such exercises; double PT sessions designed to prepare limbs for the jarring fall of parachuting; these were just some of the delights which occupied the 14 days at Hardwick.

Since their arrival, the 20 men selected by John Lander had only seen the outside of the Depot when on a forced march or when early in the morning they ran in PT shorts, vest and ammunition boots four or five miles as a preliminary warm-up for PT with rifles which followed. Inevitably this regime took its toll. Within days, the first man had been eliminated. He had dropped out, exhausted, on a forced march. There was no compassion – no second chance. Two more fell by the wayside as a result of a psychological test. 'Unsuitable' is all they would be told. For all they knew it might be anything from 'a mother complex' or 'latent homosexual tendencies' or a dozen and one other things. They would never know. Only the psychologists knew and they were not forthcoming. A man who came through all this felt that he must be pretty good.

'RTU'd' became a dreaded expression. At daily parade, RSM Strachan, made much use of this: 'If I see any more of this sloppiness, I shall personally see that the man is RTU'd', he would say. His Scottish accent was thick and caused him to draw out and curl the 'R' and cut short the 'TU'd'. Evidently some poor exhausted candidate, having been dismissed to his barrack room after a hard day, had failed to observe an approaching officer in time and had failed to march to attention and throw up the required salute in punctilious and time-honoured fashion. Happily, the officer concerned had not taken his name but had merely dropped the hint to the RSM that he should tighten up discipline if the whole Parachute Regiment was to be prevented from falling apart!

All this was, of course, a part of what Churchill would have termed 'the grand design', to instil in the men who passed through this mild purgatory that they belonged to a regiment that meant business and would accept nothing less than the first rate. Rather, one imagines, like the Brigade of Guards whose slogan 'Nulli Secondus' means 'Second to None'. Those who had already trained and done duty with good county Regiments found nothing strange in all this and were accustomed to the hard physical effort of forced marches. They were merely curious about the parachuting aspects of the course. Towards the end of the fortnight the emphasis, both mental and physical was focused on this.

There were lectures by RAF instructors on the business of parachuting: on how the parachute operated. Some learned, for the first time, that all they were required to do was hook a line to the aircraft and on a given signal, jump out and know how to fall when they met the ground. There was to be no pulling of a rip cord; no long exposed period of descent. Of course, there was more to it than that!

They were shown their first parachute and how meticulously it had to be packed; how the various 'ties' of silk thread were designed to break in the proper sequence so that, first, the 'chute would be drawn from its pack and then snap clear of its connection with the aircraft. They were shown the right and the wrong way to leave the aircraft. A bad exit could have several (all unpleasant) results.

They made their first acquaintance with such expressions as 'oscillation' and how to 'damp it down'; 'twists' and how to remedy them; 'somersaulting' and how to get the feet out of 'the rigging lines'; 'lift webs' and how to use them so as to 'face the line of drift' and phrases like 'Feet and knees together' 'Chin and elbows tucked in' 'Knees slightly bent' 'Feet canted to one side to meet the line of drift' 'Relax – roll – don't resist the impact'. The latter phrases became a sort of catechism – a ritual prayer one recited in fledgling days – an automatic reflex later.

They learned too of the fearsome 'Roman Candle', a phenomenon which, they were told, was of rare occurrence. 'How rare?' a realist wanted to know. 'Oh! Say one in ten thousand' was the instructor's reply. 'Well, those odds are good enough for me' said the questioner whose father happened to be a bookie.

The Roman Candle was, at that time, unexplained. It just happened. General opinion put it down to incorrect packing; others to static electricity causing the fabric to adhere and the parachute fail to develop; or 'thrown rigging lines' that is to say, any one or more of the 32 silk cords which sprouted from the lift webs on the parachutist's shoulders to the periphery of the parachute could come out of the pack in a way which would prevent it from opening properly. This could be due to a bad exit or bad packing.

Having been told the worst, as it were, it was emphasised that the parachute course was for volunteers only. If anyone had second thoughts about proceeding further he could sleep on it. Without any ignominy he could withdraw by handing his name into the orderly room on a slip of paper. Arrangements would then be made for his return to his original unit, without publicity.

One of John Lander's original 20 departed that way. He was present on the day's opening parade but absent for the next training session. His kit was gone from the barrack room; his bed space vacant. Later in the day his former comrades remarked: 'So old Ginger's gone then.'

'Who'd have guessed it. I thought he had all the guts in the world.'

'Perhaps he had more guts than we have. I'd face anything rather

than go back to my old mob, tail between my legs.'
'Oh! he won't go back to his old unit. They'll put him in another one.'
have. I'd face anything rather than go back to my old mob, tail between my legs.' 'Oh! he won't go back to his old unit. They'll put him in another one.'
'Yeah – the Army's pretty considerate that way.'
'Like when I applied to be posted to my brother's battalion. He was sent to the Far East and I went to Scapa Flow.'
'Well I suppose that four casualties in a fortnight isn't bad.'
'No. Old Johnny Lander sure can pick 'em, can't he. Just look at us!'

Two days later the surviving 16, along with a mixed bunch of Poles and Free French arrived at Ringway. They began what was euphemistically termed 'synthetic training'. This consisted of a lot more PT: jumping out of empty fuselages of scrapped Whitley bombers onto thick mattresses and hurling oneself off 50-feet high platforms rigged in the roof of aircraft hangers, relying on a Heath Robinson contraption called 'the Fan'.

The 'fan' itself was a sort of mill with four totally inadequate-looking blades. The theory was that the air pressure generated by the blades would allow the human body to descend at something like the same rate as would a parachute. If there was anything likely to deter one from attempting a parachute descent, it was the fiendish Fan.

Just climbing up the vertical ladder to perch on the flimsy narrow platform was awesome enough and a good test of any man's courage. To sit looking down at the all-too-small mattress 50 feet below and the upturned grinning faces waiting to witness the unceremonious dumping of one's body on the mattress from that dizzy height was something worse.

A look at the blades of the 'Fan' and at the strands of rope clipped to the harness on the jumper's back and coiled round the axis of the 'Fan' is enough to convince any sane man that this is madness. Yet when the RAF instructor shouted 'Action stations – GO' each man jumped, pushing his bottom off the narrow ledge on which it was perched. Only feet from the ground would he feel the decelerating effect of the blades of the 'Fan'. He hit the mattress pretty hard all the same. Half a dozen of these Fan drops were enough to convince a man that parachuting could only be easier!

A lot more emplaning drill and exits from the hole in the aircraft had the men ready for the real thing. In fact, a jump from an aircraft would seem like a welcome relief. The air and the soft silk of a parachute could only be kinder.

The 16 survivors were unfortunate. The time of the year was not conducive to flying. The qualifying jumps had to be sandwiched in as weather permitted. After two solid days of synthetic training they were all keyed up for their first real jumps.

They waited all Monday. Then on Tuesday the weather opened up enough for them to draw two parachutes and drive out to Tatton Park by bus to do two drops from a swaying, box-like platform suspended from a barrage balloon at 800 feet.

There was a ground mist and after ascending only 100 feet the ground could not be seen except at intervals when a slight breeze made a hole in the mist and gave a brief glimpse of the carpet of green which was Tatton Park. The ascent in the swaying balloon was frightening enough but, like the Fan, worse was to follow.

At 800 feet above the ground the balloon was brought to a stop. 'Action stations Number one.' The first of the four men to jump swung his feet into the hole with the mist-covered void between the soles of his boots and the ground.

'Go' the instructor cried sharply. Pushing himself clear of the side of the hole in the prescribed manner, Number One was on his way earthwards making his first parachute descent.

'Action stations Number two', and the next man swung his feet into the hole. The instructor steadied him. Then with a friendly tap on the shoulder said 'Go'. He went and three and four followed in the same fashion.

Before there was time to recover from the exhilaration of that first jump another parachute was fitted and senior instructors hustled the four jumpers to another waiting balloon. 'Weather's closing in, so hurry. Up 800 – five jumping.' This time the instructor will jump as well after seeing his pupils off.

Again that eerie ascent in the swaying balloon. If prone to sea or air sickness, do not go up in a balloon. This time things were really speeded up. All four sat close to the hole. 'Action stations – one – go – two – go – three – go – four – go.' In quick succession the four hopeful members of the Company exited and one after another broke through the low cloud swinging down on their developed parachutes.

When all seemed well, a bawling voice broke the peace and enchantment with an angry 'Watch your drift No. 2. Turn, man, turn. That's it. Now side right landing. Get your feet and knees together.' Number two prepared for another bone-jolting landing which has been likened to a standing jump from a 15-foot wall.

Then, full of confidence after making two parachute descents inside an hour, parachutes were rolled and carried off the DZ. A gathering at the WVS mobile canteen. Tea and a sticky bun were like nectar and ambrosia. The ladies of the WVS had seen it all before, but treated each man to a smile and made each one feel like a hero.

The weather closed in. Two days passed before it was possible to take to the air again. This time it would be in 'the flying coffin', the lumbering old Whitley. For many it would be their first flight in an aircraft. The first drop was made in slow pairs.

'Action stations No. 1 – Go.' A pause, then 'Action stations No. 2 – Go.' Then the aircraft would make another circuit before the next pair jumped. So it would continue until all ten men had left the aircraft. Dropping at 600 feet and swept back by the slipstream, the descent was noticeably shorter, the parachute seemed to open sooner, there was not the same sensation of falling as from a balloon and there was less time in which to assess the drift and to make any necessary adjustment.

One of the 16 men, hopeful material for the 21st Independent Parachute Company, landed badly in his first aircraft drop and broke an ankle. 'The blood wagon' – ever present on the edge of the DZ, rushed out from its normal station on the signal of a ground instructor. The unlucky man was quickly stowed away in the ambulance marked with its Red Cross which quickly cleared the DZ. He was seen no more. The rest of the men were unaware of what had happened and it was not until, at the end of the day and after a second flight and descent from the Whitley that some remarked 'Where's old Smithy?' 'Haven't seen him since we drew 'chutes this morning.' Then the instructor, travelling back to the barracks with these men, told them, 'Smithy, broke a leg this morning. It was hard luck but he made a lousy landing. Didn't listen well enough. Wouldn't have happened if he'd remembered "feet and knees together". Just remember that lads and you'll roll on to the "deck" very nicely every time.'

There was a small silence. 'Old Smithy' (all of 19 years of age) would not be seen again – not in the 21st, at any rate. Then someone started to whistle quietly the tune of the parachutists' song – 'When the red light goes on, we'll be ready; For the sergeant to shout "Number one" . . . .' The song was taken up by the rest of the bus load of exuberant parachute novices. Four of the seven qualifying jumps were behind them. Three more to go before they could sew the coveted blue wings and white parachute emblem on the right shoulder of their battle-dress jackets. Then, resplendent with the maroon (red) beret and neatly tailored battledress, there would be the promised seven days' leave.

Back at Larkhill, Bob Wilson asked: 'I suppose you'll be sending them on leave as soon as they arrive, John?' 'Yes – well, we'll arrange that, of course,' wheezed Johnny Lander, screwing his eyes up in characteristic fashion, 'but I've got the promise of a couple of aircraft for Friday night. I'd like 'em to do a night drop just to round 'em off. Then they can go on leave on the Saturday. That all right with you?'

This was typical of Major Lander. If the aircraft were available – use them. They were none too plentiful and his one idea was to get his unit ready for action in double quick time. For just exactly what – no one quite knew. It was largely due to him that an eighth (night) drop was added to the qualifying requirement before a man could claim his 'wings'.

The 1st Parachute Brigade were already in action in North Africa. The 3rd Battalion had dropped on the airfield at Bone on 12 November: 1st Battalion near Souk el Arba on 16 November and 2nd Battalion near Pont du Fahs on 29 November. Now in December 1942 all three battalions were fighting as infantry ahead of 1st Army among the hills of Tunisia in an endeavour to relieve pressure on 8th Army in its westward drive to push the enemy out of Africa. In the process they were earning for themselves and ultimately, for all who wore the red beret of airborne troops, the *nom de guerre* 'Die Rote Teufeln' ('the Red Devils'), which the enemy bestowed on them. It was a name which those who followed in the footsteps of those first three great battalions were proud to inherit and, by their subsequent actions, to justify.

The likelihood was that the newly formed Air Landing Brigade (gliderborne) and the 2nd Parachute Brigade consisting of the 4th, 5th (Scottish) and 6th (Welsh) Parachute Battalions, as well as Divisional troops such as the 21st Independent Parachute Company, would join the 1st Parachute Brigade in North Africa. On the other hand, 1st Parachute Brigade could as easily be flown back to Britain for a strike against the enemy in occupied Europe.

Already the Russian wolves in the shape of Joe Stalin were

howling for a Second Front in Europe. In reality, it was far too early for this to happen. Churchill and his advisors knew this, but the average member of the 21st Independent Parachute Company was not in this privileged position. He would go where he was ordered – and think about it afterwards – if there was to be 'an afterwards'.

2 LARKHILL
Winter and Spring 1942/43

The Larkhill barracks lie on sloping ground overlooking Stonehenge, that ancient monument dating back to the days of the Druids and the 18th century BC or even earlier according to some authorities. The Pathfinders came to know (and some to loathe) this venerable collection of stones very well. At the end of any route march they were always the first sign of 'home'. They would appear in one's vision on the long straight Roman road from the west and seem never to get any nearer at the end of a long and tiring march. They featured often enough in night exercises when, armed with a map, a dimmed torch and a compass, men would be dropped at various unknown spots on Salisbury Plain and told to find their own way back to barracks.

These exercises might last from 10 o'clock at night until 04.00 hours next morning depending on the number of map reference calling points that had to be made in between. Aircraft were scarce and so the 'drop' would often be simulated by putting men off in pairs from a covered truck at various points. Major Lander, Captain Wilson and Lt. Spivey would be prowling about the Plain to detect sound and give-away light flashes. They would criticise performance at an indoor session next day.

The men of the 21st came to know Salisbury Plain like the backs of their hands. They came to know the shape and size of every copse and undulation so that often, navigating only by the stars, they could be back in the Larkhill barracks, snug under their rough Army blankets in half the time they might have taken weeks before. To make life more difficult NCO's would be sent out in daylight to plot a point-to-point course on compass bearings and giving stated distances between each point. Clues would be left in hidden tins to lead men on to the next leg of the course.

Occasionally, aircraft in small numbers would be made available for parachute drops to be made. Exercises would then be carried out using the aids for bringing in other aircraft and symbolic follow-up drops would be made with containers or dummy parachutists.

The usual dropping zone (DZ) would be in the area of that delightful Wiltshire village, Berwick St. James. Men would clamour to take part in these drops. They were keen to add to their parachute experience. The fact that 'mine host' at the beautiful old Tudor style village pub would close his eyes to 'closing time' on these occasions may have had something to do with it! The local policeman, conscientious enough in making his nightly rounds on a bicycle, would also contrive not to be around that vicinity when he heard the drone of aircraft from across the Plain at Netheravon. 'Arr – the boys'll be dropping tonight. Best be going to see what's to do up the road towards . . . ' he tailed off not saying which way he was going. And the landlord would know it would be all right to serve the mud-stained, camouflage-smocked parachutists in the back snug-parlour, even after hours.

They would come in, having dumped their rolled up parachutes in the three-tonner truck waiting to take them back to barracks, laughing and talking about the drop they had just made and make the landlord feel he was part of the war-effort, as indeed he was. 'Something went wrong with that one, didn't it. I was no more than 300 feet off the deck – parachute only just opened – then I hit the deck.' 'Reckon there was something wrong with the bloody altimeter or else the navigator didn't take into account that rise.' They had been dropped that night in a ground mist on sloping ground not far from the pub. 'Couldn't see the ground — had a horrible backward landing – could have broke my neck.' 'All in a day's work – wouldn't have missed it for worlds'. These and similar remarks, sometimes expressed more forcibly, flew across the close smokey atmosphere of the snuggery until a sergeant's voice came breaking up the party. 'OK lads – drink up – truck's leaving in two minutes.' Quick gulps and goodnights to the landlord, then out into the cold night air and back to barracks.

At this time, just before Christmas 1942, the Company was by no means yet at full strength. They numbered perhaps no more than 60 including the three officers. Batches of new arrivals fresh from their parachute course would arrive at roughly fortnightly intervals. Platoon strengths and complements were still being worked out; experiments were always being made to determine the nature of the navigational aids which were to be carried and methods by which they were to be transported to the scene of action.

A squad of men would go out, with one of the officers, in a lorry taking with them various types of markers to lay out on the ground in some isolated part of Salisbury Plain. Major Lander and some of the men would then fly with either Whitley or glider crews to observe the efforts from the air. On other occasions Major Lander would set an exercise which required a stick of parachutists to drop with the equipment they were to use. Their performance would be timed from the time they landed to the moment all aids were laid out and all-round protection given to the site.

It was very early decided that the use of containers for the carrying of these aids was unsatisfactory. The heavy metal cylinders were difficult to pack and to load into bomb-bays where they had to be perfectly balanced if, as so often happened, they were not to be caught up in the bomb-bays and fail to arrive or be so delayed in dropping that they landed far away from the men who were to use their contents.

John Lander personally experimented with alternative means of transporting the not inconsiderable weight of equipment needed for the job. He finally hit on the simple device of jumping his men with a kitbag loaded with equipment (anything up to 60 pounds in weight) strapped, at first to both legs but soon to the right leg only. After the man's parachute had opened he would pull a quick release and lower the kitbag to the end of a twenty-foot rope securely tied to his webbing waist belt. There it would hang, land a split second before the parachutist and be ready to hand as soon as the man landed and shed his parachute. It was found that this gave the man a smoother ride down and, usually, a softer landing. In very still air there was, of course, always the possibility of landing awkwardly on top of the kitbag. This did not often happen.

The weight of the kitbag suspended 20 feet below the man tended to cut down oscillation (the swing of the man below the parachute) and the sudden lessening of weight for the parachute to support as soon as the kitbag hit the ground first, also tended to give a cushioning effect to the man's own landing.

There was a limit to the number of men in a stick who could jump with a kitbag because of its hampering effect on the speed of exit. Speedy exits from the aircraft were essential to ensure close distribution of men on the ground. Using Whitleys, with their well-like holes in the floor to jump from, meant that only the first two men, perched on either side of the hole for practically the whole of the flight, could jump encumbered with a kitbag lashed to both legs.

Later, when the idea of securing the bag to only one leg was tried out, it was found that three and sometimes four could perform this task. Still later, when the much more accommodating Dakota aircraft was available, with its door and stand up exit, it was a matter of comparative ease for the first four men, closely grouped at the door, to jump in rapid succession. The rest of the stick following, carrying their usual arms and equipment would all be down along with the kitbag men within a space of a few hundred yards and be able quickly to link up on the ground to perform their several tasks. The task itself varied slightly according to whether a parachute dropping zone (DZ) or a glider landing zone (LZ) was to be marked.

Basically, this consisted of locating a little radio-beacon, Eureka, more or less in the centre of the selected area, but enough off centre to take account of wind direction; the laying out of the distinguishing letter of the DZ or LZ and the provision of a ground 'T' to ensure that aircraft and gliders flew into the wind for the landing. By day different coloured smoke canisters were ignited immediately before the main body of troops dropped.

The equipment used to do the marking consisted of white nylon panels about a metre wide and four metres long, each weighted with steel rods. Four or five of these would be needed to form the distinguishing letter and another half dozen for the 'T'. Add the Eureka set and smoke canisters. Duplicate the lot as insurance against the failure of one aircraft to arrive and already there was enough gear to require at least six kitbags. Throw in Bren guns and loaded magazines and at least three more were needed for a Platoon task.

So much for a daylight operation. A night zone marking was even more burdensome. Instead of panels it was necessary to use lights. Here was another great source of experimentation, trial and tribulation. The problem of reasonably handy lights with sufficient power to have any meaning to pilots anything up to ten miles away at heights which might vary from a few hundred feet in the case of parachute carriers and a thousand feet or more in the case of gliders, was never really solved, at least to the Pathfinders' satisfaction.

What did evolve was admirable from the air and it worked; but the burden of the 21st Independent Parachute Company was increased enormously. Heavy lamps specially made of thick shatterproof glass, long lengths of heavy-service rubber-clad electric cable and 12-volt car batteries made up the load and took the place of the nylon panels. The lamps were called 'Glim' lamps. They were designed so that no light showed from them at ground level, the reflectors were angled so as only to be visible from the right height and angle in the sky. They had to be placed correctly in the open so as not to be obscured by trees or low hills. Setting them up naturally took rather longer than laying out panels in daylight. The time lag between the landing of the pathfinders and arrival of the main body was therefore anything up to an hour for a night operation as opposed to the half hour or 20 minutes for one in daylight.

The key to the whole business was the getting of the pathfinder force to the area of operations with accuracy and without ground aids such as they themselves carried. For this purpose 38 Wing trained its navigators to the nth degree and the Company came to have the utmost confidence in them.

The second key factor was the magic box 'Eureka', well-named indeed as one could easily imagine the navigator of the leading aircraft in a mass formation re-echoing the words of Archimedes 'I have found it!'. Training and experiment in the use of this equipment continued throughout the hard winter of 1942.

A glider pilot (Lawrence Wright author of *The Wooden Sword*) recalls that a Whitley flew one night across its home airfield at 300 feet, in full moon, while the flare-path and obstruction lights were lit. Its navigator, trusting 'Rebecca' (Eureka's responding partner in the aircraft) above eyesight, dropped eight unhappy paratroops on the roofs surrounding the Signals Section, where a Eureka set, under repair, had been left on!

Of the experiment he records: 'Dropping Lander in the dark, we would give him 20 minutes to set up Eureka; then we would send the squadron in to drop dummy parachutes from each aircraft; Lander would note their positions. Daily after breakfast we met to study results. I had drawn concentric circles on a cyclostyled diagram on which we plotted each night's work. The accuracy was fantastic; within a few days the 1000 yard circle had to be re-scaled as a 100 yard circle and every dummy was usually well inside it.'

'From the nose of one of the Whitleys,' Wright adds, 'I once had a glimpse of Lander running to evade a dummy that nearly smashed the Eureka by which he had stood.' Of Lander himself, Wright says, 'He still showed that terrifying energy. Having flown in the front turret on a sortie, he returned before midnight and thus in time to go to a dance. At nine next morning, I had occasion to consult him and to leave a message against his awakening. "The Major isn't here" the orderly room clerk informed me. I was not surprised. "He's gone on a route march" the clerk added!'

The clerk was probably either Lance Corporal 'Red' McGee or Ben Swallow, whose early job was to do the necessary paperwork to put the Company together and get it under way. Headquarters Platoon in those early days included SSM Jackson (APTC), CQMS Lax (famous for his wry sense of humour), 'Ginger' Green, the storeman, and McCluskey, orderly room runner. McCluskey was not long with the Company and he would never have made a parachutist. No more would Corporal 'Jerry' Gordon of the Army Catering Corps who looked after the Company's 'inner man' to such good effect that he served with it right through until 1945 in Norway. Corporal (later Sergeant) Gordon was more than a good cook – he was also a magician. This only came to light much later.

It will be appreciated that HQ Platoon included a number of attached Corps personnel, who varied from time to time. Those who cared saw to it that they stayed. Among these was Sergeant 'Nick' Carter (REME) who could unerringly 'zero' the rifles, service the Stens and put right the PIATs of the Company.

For Christmas 1942 Corporal Christie, a talented photographer, produced the Company's own Christmas card. It incorporated three parachutists jumping from a Whitley, the badge of the Army Air Corp (later only worn by glider pilots) – this was before the Parachute Regiment badge was devised – and a banner reading '21st Independent Parachute Company Xmas 1942'. Christie left the Company to join the Army Photographic Unit which did such good work covering the D-Day landings and the Arnhem operation.

Christie was a 'Puckish' character – very popular with such

pals as 'Beau' Bowditch, Bill Dawkins (not to be confused with 'Lofty' Dawkins), Archie Mansell, 'Dutch' Holland, Stan Sullivan, Solly Solomon and many others of the old original Company. Though it has proved impossible to compose a complete roster of all those who were the first comers to the Company it is certain that many of them had had previous flying experience. They were, in fact, potential glider pilots who, after a bare eight broken hours of flying instruction in Tiger Moths, had been rejected because they had not 'gone solo' in that time. Parallel courses for bomber pilots had up to 15 hours in which to 'go solo'. Amongst these 'rejects' – first-class material – they had passed the exacting health and physique requirements of the RAF – were such men as Bill Price, Frank Buck, Ken Philipson and Ron Kent – the last three all from the Royal Sussex Regiment.

Many enlisted by John Lander held war-substantive ranks as NCO's and were specialist instructors in weapons, field craft, map reading, physical training and unarmed combat. All except a few were required to relinquish all rank in order to join John Lander's pathfinder company. Among the excepted few was Sonny Binick. He had only to drop from Company Sergeant Major to Sergeant. He became and remained Platoon Sergeant of No. 1 Platoon. Before the war he had been a professional ballroom dancer and champion. Val Allerton was another who came in as Sergeant in charge of No. 2 Platoon. But these were exceptions and there were many who, very competent weapon instructors and infantry leaders, reverted to the rank of private but quickly regained their rank on merit.

One intake included a whole section of Irishmen from the Royal Inniskilling Fusiliers. Sergeant 'Slim' Summerville was their conducting NCO, a young veteran who had been through the ordeal of evacuation from Dunkirk. With him were such promising young soldiers as Danny Gillespie, Paddy Gamble, Tommy Scullion, Jimmy Cameron and Paddy Cockings.

As if to ensure the cosmopolitan character of the Company John Lander introduced a strong contingent of Jewish ex-refugees from Hitler's Germany and Austria. Chosen for their fluency in both German and English these men proved to be magnificent in action. We shall hear more of them as this history unfolds. They had all taken on new names to avoid identification if they were captured. Many of the names chosen were Scottish and all their army papers were made out in those names. In fact their comrades in arms knew them by no other. There were the

Bruces, I and II, Melford, Rodley, Landon, McManus and a number of others. Still more were to join later. There were no fewer than 25 on the Company strength by the time the Arnhem operation was carried out. All highly intelligent, they proved to have great fighting qualities and had more reason than the rest of the Company for giving vent to their hatred of the enemy.

Because of the very special nature of the company they had joined; the feeling of having been chosen – singled out as it were, there was, right from the beginning, a very real and close bond of comradeship amongst all ranks. It was something which grew and strengthened as more and more experiences were shared. There was about the Company an intangible *esprit de corps*, difficult to express but nevertheless there to be felt and sensed by any newcomer.

As the winter of 1942/43 progressed much time was spent indoors, in make-shift classrooms, working at blackboard exercises on map reading, navigation by the stars, the Morse code, the laying-out pattern and method for the pathfinder task itself. There were also weapon-training sessions, but a minimum of barrack square drill and, best of all, no guard duties. At worst there were in-lying fire piquets nominated for the weekends. Weekend passes were fairly freely available and there were Saturday afternoon and evening trips into Salisbury to look forward to. During the week there was the NAAFI canteen and the Garrison cinema to share with the Company's near neighbour, the 6th (Welsh) Parachute Battalion, of whom little was otherwise seen.

The Company was left very much to its own devices, but Major Lander saw to it that it kept busy. There was great emphasis on physical fitness and the excellent gymnasium at Larkhill was in use every day. Unarmed combat and silent killing methods were taught and practised; team games such as hand- and volley-ball were played and keenly contested. As the weather improved night exercises were recommenced, with small map-reading teams finding their way about Salisbury Plain. A live exercise with glider landings was carried out just south of Larkhill close by the venerable pile of massive stones which is Stonehenge.

John Lander had an obsession about Stonehenge. Maybe his ancient ancestors had been Druids! On one occasion he took the whole Company into Salisbury for a learned discourse on the history and meaning of this temple of Druids, and most of the Company at some time or other spent some time in and around the huge formation of stones.

In the second week of February 1943 sufficient aircraft (all Whitleys) were made available for the Company, for the first time, to take to the air together. At dawn on 11 February the Company descended on the open fields above the White Horse Hill overlooking Osmington Mills not far from Weymouth. There were coastal batteries at Osmington Mills and the Company took on a different role. No longer acting as pathfinders, it was to test the local defences. The attack was anything but a concerted one. It ignored all the rules of 'the Company in the attack' and it was left to individual section leaders to probe the defences. It was more an exercise for the defence than for the attack. For the Company it was just one more parachuting experience – a practice in jumping in an unknown spot, in forming up in sections and descending from the high ground on which the drop had taken place and in map reading and the choice of covered approaches. The defence consisted of a battalion of infantry and some local Home Guards. There were some umpires who had the irritating habit of appearing with their red arm bands and white flags, giving away our covered approach lines to say, 'You are under machine gun fire' and sometimes, only as an afterthought, 'From the corner of that wood over there'. It was all rather dull because we hardly saw the enemy until the exercise was almost at an end and theoretically we were all 'put in the bag' only to be given a good hot meal of 'M & V' (meat and veg.). The exercise lasted from dawn until midday.

By 14.00 hours the Company was on its way back to Larkhill – on foot. With the best part of 60 miles to cover, it was a case of best foot forward and keep going; out of Dorset and into Wiltshire, heading north-east for Stonehenge and Larkhill.

Twenty-four hours later, after a mere four hours rest in the barns of a farm near Sixpenny Handley and a hot meal provided by Corporal Gordon and his crew brought by Company transport from Larkhill, the Company came within sight of Stonehenge miles away on the long straight stretch of road from the west. 'A welcome sight, eh, Corporal Kent?' Major Lander pacing alongside No. 1 Platoon, chuckled. 'I wouldn't care if I never saw those stones ever again, sir,' was the tired response. It had been a very tiring 36 hours since the Company had taken off at 04.00 hours on the 11th until its arrival at Larkhill on the afternoon of the 12th. And it rained.

A shower, dry clothes, a high tea served in the cookhouse by

Corporal Gordon – sausage and mash and hot sweet tea, bread
and jam – all very welcome. Foot inspection – 'Doc' Toms and
'Doc' Taylor RAMC popping a few blisters and wiping them
with a swab of aqua flavin. Then CQMS Lax decided to have a
kit inspection. Highly critical of the state of socks, he took the
opportunity to exercise his sense of humour. Viewing one pair,
sweat stained and muddied, practically standing up on their
own, CQMS Lax muttered 'Put them in for studding'. He
laughed immoderately at his own joke and passed on, oblivious
of the pitying looks the owner of the socks and his immediate
neighbours bestowed on him. CQMS Lax had not been on that
march and was not too much admired at that moment.

Presently some bright spark in the RAF had the idea that a
Halifax bomber might make a suitable aircraft for paratroops to
drop from and devised a hole similar to the one in the Whitley
for the poor old parachutist to jump out of. It fell to No. 1
Platoon to provide a stick of ten to do an experimental jump
from one of these four-engined monsters. The biggest snag to a
Halifax as a parachute carrier was the fact that it had a
split-level floor to its fuselage and the hole was situated in the
lower after level. Added to this it could carry only four equipped
men aft of the hole; the rest had to sit on the floor above and
forward of the hole.

The men selected for the jump were all fairly experienced and
reckoned to be some of the fastest jumpers. Corporal Kent and
most of his section, the Irishmen, Tommy Scullion, Danny
Gillespie, Paddy Gamble, Jimmy Cameron were some of them.
Ideally, an aircraft dropping parachutists should have a low
stalling speed. It should be capable of dropping to an airspeed of
something like 90 miles an hour as the men leap out. Higher
speeds than that can do funny things to parachutes and to the
body movements of the men as they exit.

The lowest speed the Halifax could achieve without dropping
out of the sky was 120 miles an hour. Over Berwick St. James
the red light came on and the first to jump perched high above
the frightening looking hole. It was daylight and the dun-
coloured ground rushed by below. The green light came on and
No. 1 hopped down from his perch and shot his feet into the
centre of the hole and disappeared down the well. No. 2 from aft
of the hole followed. No. 3 from forward – No. 4 from aft and so
on until Nos. 9 and 10 eventually cleared the aircraft from
forward. It was not a fast stick chiefly because of the
split-second delay of having to drop down on to the platform

from forward of the hole. The stick of ten was spread over nearly a mile. Not good enough, it was decided, and the Halifax was shelved as a carrier of regular parachutists. It might have been used for dropping SAS, Resistance and irregular agents, but the Company was not asked to use it again until Palestine.

It is a fact that the British never once introduced an aircraft particularly suited to parachuting until after the war, when the Hastings carrier came into operation. It was perhaps understandable, in wartime, to utilise what one had, bombers and fighter bombers. Our American allies brought us the C.47, the Dakota, an aircraft the Company was not to make use of until it found itself in North Africa.

By the end of April the Company was building up to full strength and it had gained a new Sergeant Major. CSM Jackson APTC was replaced by a young Regular soldier, Chris Keirnan who had been in the Army since boyhood. He proved to be just what the Company needed and was very popular, but he stood no nonsense from the high-spirited unit he had inherited.

Whilst still at Larkhill the Company had a week or two of a pantomime called 'Battle Drill'. The idea behind this drill was sound enough, but it did seem ridiculous to parade on a barrack square to carry out to drill movements the principles of 'fire and movement'. It entailed a section or platoon, solemnly advancing in extended order, being halted by the command 'You are under fire'. Each man was then required to shout at the top of his voice 'Down, crawl, observe, fire', then work the bolt action of his rifle or sten gun to simulate firing. The section leader was then required to decide whether to go left or right of the obstructing enemy. 'I am going left flanking' (or right flanking, as the case might be). 'Bren gun give covering fire – rifle section – follow me.' The Bren crew would remain static to give the necessary covering fire and the section leader would march his riflemen off to the left in single file. At a suitable distance from the Bren gun he would take a right-angled turn to the right, march a suitable distance to where he judged he was in a position on the flank of the offending enemy post. 'Right turn' and he and the rifle section would face into line. 'Fix bayonets – bullets'. The opening of fire from the flank was a signal to the Bren section to be ready to cease fire as soon as the charge went in. 'Rifle section – advance'. The rifle section was required to do so at the high port position, that is to say, with the rifle canted across the body at an angle of 45°. On the word 'Charge', the rifles were swung down, the horizontal bayonets thrust forward menacingly. 'Bullets, bullets' came next – the charge was going in – riflemen firing from the hip. The covering fire ceased – the position overrun – riflemen went through and beyond the position ('Never consolidate on the enemy position') to take up a forward defence position. The Bren gun then moved up to its old position on the section's flank and the exercise was complete.

Now all this was carried out to drill movements and words of command. It might be very well to instil elementary battle tactics into average infantrymen, but to the men of the 21st Independent Parachute Company it was a rather solemn farce, not to be taken too seriously. The highly intelligent and imaginative men required to carry out this (to them) ludicrous exercise were highly critical of it all in the barrack rooms later.

'What happens if you run into another enemy post once you've parted company with the Bren?' 'How do you keep contact with your Bren in close country?' These and many other related questions were fired at NCOs who had had this drill wished upon them and were supposed to impart it to their men. They knew no more than the men did. Still, if it had no other effect it stimulated thought and the men of the Company began to work out their own ideas for dealing with the confrontation situation.

During these months considerable thought had been given to the Company's ultimate war strength and composition. It eventually emerged that the Company would be composed, like any infantry company, of three platoons and a headquarters platoon and that it should have an establishment of 180 NCOs and other ranks and six officers. There might from time to time be *ad hoc* attachments from other units as circumstances required but that was the strength aimed at.

Each platoon would be led by a full lieutenant and would have the usual four infantry sections (including platoon headquarters); beside the platoon sergeant there would be three other sergeants, each leading a section. Because of the unusual nature and responsibility of the Company's task each platoon would have an unusually high complement of NCOs. Each section would have both a full corporal and a lance-corporal to assist the section sergeant. Thus each section had or was to have three NCOs and a further seven to nine other ranks according to the job to be done. A section might therefore consist of as many as a dozen men, three of whom would be NCOs. A platoon might thus consist of up to 48 in action, including attached Signals and

Medical Corps men and perhaps an Army Catering Corps cook.

This arrangement left a fairly large numbered Company Headquarters comprising the OC, 2I/C and Adjutant, a Signals Officer, an Intelligence Officer and sometimes a Medical Officer, each with the attendant staff of clerks, orderlies and batman, all of whom (apart from the medics) would be expected to be active in defence of headquarters in any action, along with a defence team led by the Company Sergeant Major. Included in the Company headquarters strength were the non-parachuting second echelon comprising heavy transport drivers, Company cooks, the CQMS and storemen. Others attached to headquarters were the sergeant armourer and his assistant, a Signals sergeant and several Royal Corps of Signals personnel to handle the larger communications sets.

Inter platoon and inter Company communications were catered for with '38' sets and 'walkie-talkies', the latter having limited range especially in close country. It will be seen that whilst the basic structure of the Company was that of an ordinary infantry company its infra-structure was on a more generous scale and Company headquarters was something approaching that of a battalion HQ. This was because pre-operational planning made special demands and in action platoons might well be acting in areas as widely separated as infantry companies in relation to their battalion HQ. Indeed, there were many occasions when platoons operated quite independent of and far distant from Company headquarters, according to the nature of the tasks assigned.

Quite apart from its pathfinder role, the Company had a secondary role once its pathfinder duties were done. They came directly under the Divisional commander or, if the operation was at only Brigade strength, the Brigadier. In General Browning's early conception the Company would become his defence Company in any major action but would otherwise be at the disposal of the commander in the field for 'special tasks'.

The Company was therefore trained not only in its pathfinder role but in every aspect of infantry work specialising in field craft, small arms and map reading. Every man was a very good shot and many were first-class marksmen. Every section had its specialist sniper complete with his carefully zero'ed rifle and sniper's sight. NCOs were trained to absolute proficiency in the use of automatic weapons, especially the Browning automatic pistol, the short-ranged Sten and German weapons which might be captured. In Italy at least one sergeant was to hand in his Sten gun to the CQMS in preference for the superior German Schmeisser he captured. Both fired standard 9mm. ammunition and the Schmeisser had a longer range, was more reliable and less subject to the touchy faults of the early Sten.

A long day's shoot on the ranges near Bulford would bring its aftermath of friendly rivalry for the coveted role of sniper, and individual scores would be carefully analysed. Equally, Bren gunners would vie with each other for the reputation of top gunner in the Company.

At a very early stage in the formation of the three operational platoons a healthy belief in the superiority of one's own platoon grew up. No. 1 Platoon liked to think that it was the leading platoon of the Company. In some respects it may have been. It certainly had some top notch infantrymen and parachutists. In the same way No. 2 Platoon had its own ideas on the subject, and in the line of pathfinder it was from No. 2 Platoon that Major Lander selected the men for specialist tasks. No 3 Platoon at this time was rather in its infancy but was rapidly finding its feet to vie with both No. 1 and No. 2 Platoon, both of which, under Sergeants Binick and Allerton respectively, were the first to approach combat readiness. At this time they were still without officer leadership.

What were they like and where were they from – these men, 'the originals' of the Company? Their average age would be somewhere in the early twenties; some there were who were older but not much so; others were still in their teens, but were rapidly to grow into full manhood in the next year or two. They came from all parts of the British Isles and some from further afield. There was a strong body of Londoners, many from the Home Counties, from the Midlands and from the North; there were Welshmen, Scotsmen and Irishmen.

They came from many walks of life and had varying standards of education, but all had the common denominator – parachuting; and they had mutual respect and made friends easily. Thrown together in close quarters for months at a time, they shared common discomforts and simple pleasures and seldom did animosity arise between them; when it did, it was quickly dispelled, usually with a joke or by a session with the boxing gloves in the gym.

There was friendly rivalry between the embryo platoons, engendered by the men themselves and not consciously provoked by their officers. Typical of the Scots were 'Jocks' Crighton, Moir, McKnight, McArthur and Candy Marsland; of the Welsh, there were the two Jones', Gus and 'Gremlin', the Irish have already been mentioned. The Londoners included the irrepressible 'Solly' Solomon, 'Smoky' London, 'Tex' Taylor, Jack Schofield and Tommy McMahon. From further afield there was Gordon Anderson from Cornwall and Stan Sullivan from Tyneside. Characters, every one of them, each in his own way would in the months and years to come make his contribution to the special character of the Company as a whole.

It has not, unfortunately, proved possible to compile a complete list of all who joined the Company at Larkhill, but as many names as can be traced have been included in the Nominal Roll and Index (p.167).

Towards the end of April 1943 the Company was alerted for overseas service and sent off on 'embarkation leave'. A large contingent headed for London, and Waterloo Station saw their arrival. There they split up and each went his own way either in London itself or northward or south into Kent, Sussex and Surrey, to their homes. Amongst the London contingent was one, Hobbs, very young but already making a name for himself as a character. When he had first heard that the Company was to leave England he had had his head shaved. Now that he was going on leave (to be spent with his maiden aunt who had brought him up) he could not face her with a bald head so he devised an elaborate head bandage and thought up some story about a parachute accident. To make the story more convincing he bought some plaster of Paris, scrounged a lot of bandage from the medics and with their guidance put his left arm in plaster from wrist to elbow. Looking the part of the wounded hero, he got his mates to perch his red beret on the side of his head and was off to Surrey to live a lie for seven days.

At the end of the seven days, a number of the Company assembled at Waterloo Station to catch the late-night train to Salisbury. Among the high spirited bunch who met in the rather dreary railway pub for a last beer before catching their train, was paratrooper Hobbs. He had discarded his head bandage on the way up from Surrey, but he still had his arm in plaster. In his right hand he took a table knife from time to time and shoved it between the plaster and the skin of his forearm to scratch the itch with which he had had to live whilst on leave with his aunt. He was now intent on shedding the plaster. He tried bashing it on the back of a chair, much to the astonishment of other soldiers and civilians in the pub, but to rousing encouragement from his red-bereted companions. Eventually, accompanied by two or three enthusiastic assistants, he retired to the stark, tiled toilets of Waterloo Station. He emerged some ten minutes later – just in time to catch the last train – free of the plaster, but with his escort displaying various fragments of porcelain sanitary ware, sad casualty of the assault upon it that Hobbs, in his desperation, felt driven to. It must have been little incidents like this which gave civilians and others the impression of para-trooper toughness and eccentricity. The Company regarded it as a pretty good joke.

It is appropriate at this point to outline the background against which the Company spent its months of preparation for action. Although in the Deserts of North Africa it looked as though the war was turning in the favour of the Allies, the Germans remained firmly entrenched in 'Fortress Europa' and the end of the war was still a long way off, with many battles and campaigns still to be fought. The Battle of El Alamein opened on 23 October, 1942 and Operation 'Torch' was launched by a combined British and American Army on 8 November. The former battle was the beginning of a relentless advance by the 8th Army upon Rommel's Afrika Korps and the Italian Army from the east. 'Torch' was the landing of the 1st Allied Army in Morocco and Algeria with the object of bringing pressure to bear on the enemy from the west. As the 1st and 8th Armies converged there was every hope of cutting off and defeating a large part of Germany's best fighting units, their armour and supplies. A lightning strike by 1st Army into Tunisia before the North African winter set in might see the end of German resistance there by the end of the year; the knocking out of the war of the Italians was also forseeable.

On the Russian Front, the Russians were also striking back and on 23 November closed the circle around General von Paulus' Sixth German Army in the Stalingrad area of oper-ations. On 31 January, 1943 von Paulus was forced to surrender, all hope of a relief column reaching him having been abandoned. 90,000 prisoners were taken by the Russians, the survivors of 21 German and one Roumanian Division.

The winter of 1942/43 was particularly severe both in Russia and in North Africa, where impossible road and communication conditions brought the advances from east and west to a standstill. It was recognised that final victory in North Africa could only be gained in the spring of 1943 at earliest. Nevertheless, there was still talk in the highest command circles of 'crossing the Channel in 1943' and of 'building up in Great

Britain' a force of 1,100,000 men for 'Bolero' (Churchill, *The Second World War*, Vol 8, p. 216). In January 1943 the Chiefs of Staff Committee still recorded in their minutes a policy proposal in which, whilst exploiting 'Torch' as vigorously as possible, 'there should be a build-up. of "Bolero" on the greatest scale . . . in order that we be ready to re-enter the Continent with about 21 divisions in August or September 1943, if the conditions are such that there is a good prospect of success.' (*ibid* p. 234). On the Russian side, Stalin was pressing for an even earlier opening of a Second Front in Europe.

Even the rank and file of troops in Britain realised that that did not appear at all feasible. The Americans had been in the war for more than a year by January 1943, but apart from the landings in North Africa as part of the 'Torch' operation (where by all accounts they showed themselves to be pretty 'green'), they were thought to be doing little more than invade Britain with over-paid, loud-mouthed troops, some 20,000 air and ground crew and 500 aircraft, not one of which in the last six months of 1942 had dropped a single bomb on Germany by their daylight-bombing methods.

The general feeling was that what had been so well started in North Africa should be brought to a swift and successful conclusion as soon as possible in the New Year and, from that base, see a logical re-entry into Europe from the Mediterranean seaboard rather than from across the English Channel. Did it really matter where the enemy was engaged in Europe? So long as he was engaged, and engaged on a large scale, the relieving effect on the Russian Front would be the same.

So the argument went, but Stalin and those in the Company who had some sympathy with what we were told of the Russians' stiff opposition to the German, held other views. The shortest route into Germany itself was through France and across the Rhine. Only when Germans were forced to fight on their own soil would the war be brought home to them and, it was thought, would more readily collapse. Still others felt that the Germans would not be so easily driven and would resist the harder with their backs to the wall in their own land unless they had first been softened up internally by intense bombing of cities and war-production centres and their armies depleted and divided on a whole series of fronts.

It says something for the calibre of some men in the Company that they were capable of this kind of strategic debate. This is not to say that much time was given to such discussions: most of the time was taken up with their own immediate problems and exertions. Still, casual conversations on these lines did take place in the barrack rooms, on route marches and in the canteen.

On 23 January 1943 the 8th Army entered Tripoli and not long after this it became known that the Allied leaders had decided on a policy of 'Unconditional Surrender' in dealing with the Axis Powers. At the time many of the Company felt that such a policy could only prolong the war as it left the enemy no hope of a negotiated peace and their resistance would be all the stiffer. Such a policy could only be effective if the Allies had the means to make life so intolerable for the enemy that he would give up merely to preserve his life. At that point of the war the average soldier had no evidence that the Allies had such overwhelming superiority. Although he was beginning to appreciate that America had vast material resources, he had yet to see them brought into effective use, and there was little reason to feel confident in America's ability to do so. Subsequent experience of the Americans at first hand in the year ahead did little to increase that confidence. In fact many of the Company came to dislike actively the GI's they met in Salisbury and Saturday nights in the town frequently resulted in hand-to-hand fighting, most of which was regarded as good sport. Some of it may have been engendered by sheer boredom and for want of something better to do after a few beers. Certainly there was a feeling that it was about time that we went somewhere and got into the war.

Embarkation for overseas was, therefore, welcomed and it was evident that the Company looked forward to a change of scene and some action in a foreign land. There was about the Company a spirit of boyish thirst for adventure. It was never expressed as such and if put to them in those terms would have been debunked in no uncertain terms. It was there all the same.

Before leaving England, the Company, along with the Air-landing Brigade and the 2nd Parachute Brigade, were reviewed by King George VI on the open slopes above the camp at Bulford.

The Company was about to be launched out into the Atlantic *en route* for North Africa at a time when the U-boat menace was still at its height. In March 1943 the Allies had lost 97 ships in the first 20 days alone. In April it was known that there were 98 German submarines waiting for victims, but the Navy was gradually winning the Battle of the Atlantic. During the month it accounted for seven U-boats and the tally of ships lost was reduced to 56 totalling 330,000 tons. It was not until the following month that the turning point of the war at sea was reached. As background to the Company's first excursion outside England, Anthony Cave Brown's *Bodyguard of Lies* makes interesting reading.

3 NORTH AFRICA
'High Hopes'

Towards the end of April 1943 the Company, in common with the rest of the division, prepared to join the 1st Brigade in North Africa. 1st Brigade had been in North Africa since its leading elements had been flown there via Gibraltar in November 1942. All three battalions of this fine Parachute Brigade had seen plenty of action against the Germans in, on and around the hills of Tunisia, throughout the winter of 1942/43. They had distinguished themselves in no uncertain fashion and earned the name 'Red Devils' which was later applied to the 1st Airborne Division as a whole and later still to all who wore the red beret of British Airborne Forces.

These were the men the Company was now to join. It took a long ten days at sea out of Liverpool before the Company landed at Oran in Algeria. Those ten days spent in the confined space of a troopship in convoy far out into the Atlantic cured many a man from wanting to go to sea again. The time was spent in a routine of mess-deck inspections, fatigues, daily boat drill, PT sessions and queuing for rations of tobacco, cigarettes and sweets when the canteen opened for an hour twice a day.

Card games and housey-housey sessions filled in the evenings. Most were reluctant to go below at night to sleep in hammocks stacked in three layers in the crowded mess decks. There were occasional submarine alarms and from the deck of the troopship the escort vessels could be seen and heard dropping depth charges. Once a German Condor on its reconnaissance flight out of occupied France was seen high in the sky.

After being out of sight of land for day after monotonous day, with nothing but a heaving sea to look at, there came a moment when, passing through the Straits of Gibraltar, the Company feasted its collective eyes on 'The Rock' on the one hand and its first view of Africa on the other. The landfall gleamed golden in the sunlight; the sea sparkled an azure welcome as only the Mediterranean can. A ripple of excited anticipation ran through the Company which was heightened as it approached the port of Oran, with its dazzling white façade of buildings around and above the quayside.

Oran had been the scene of drama when, faced with capture, the Vichy French fleet had decided to scuttle itself. Here and there could be seen the remains of scuttled ships, their superstructures showing just above the water level. Nosing its way through these wrecks, the troopship took its time to dock. It was during this interval that the Company received its first whiff of the smell so characteristic of northern Africa from Morocco right through to Egypt. It is a smell which conjures up pictures of camels, donkeys and white shrouded Arabs. It is a warm, heavy smell, not unpleasant at a distance and mingled with the ozone of the sea.

The Company was transported from the docks of Oran to a tented transit camp some miles away, between Fleurus and St. Cloud, in US Army trucks driven by American negroes, the first the Company had seen. On bare open slopes of red sand the Company drew up its lines and erected tents, finding itself neighbours of American infantry units. The Company started on its daily dose of Mepacrin, those tiny yellow pills which, if taken regularly, successfully prevented malaria, but also turned the skin a distinctly Oriental colour in spite of the tan from the sun.

No sooner arrived than the CO (wisely no doubt) decided that a route march would be a healthy thing! Another followed early on the morning after the Company's first few hours' liberty run into Oran. This was something of a disappointment and disaster for some. There was little else to do there but sample the local rough red wine which was cheap and plentiful enough. Some who over-indulged lived to regret it and had 'the trots' for days after. Besides this, some thought they were sweating blood on the route march next day. It was probably a combination of sweat and the stain of the fine red sand which caused this discolouration of the khaki drill tropical uniform the Company now wore.

Not more than a week later the Company struck camp and

moved south, again in US Army trucks, through Mascara, passing the turn-off to the home of the French Foreign Legion at Sidi Bel Abbes and finally settling in the vicinity of an airstrip near the village of Froha. Company lines were again set up in tents. Life in this part of Africa was anything but enchanting. Dust, flies mosquitoes and chlorinated water are not the best of companions.

It was not until the second week of June (the Company had arrived in Algeria on 19 May) that a limited number of aircraft was made available to the Company: sufficient only to enable a platoon at a time to carry out parachute exercises. Then some of the Company were able to do two or even three jumps inside a week. There was much competition for these welcome breaks in the otherwise dull routine of camp life.

Albemarles were the new aircraft from which the Company now jumped for the first time. They were cramped, allowing only sticks of ten, the first two jumping with kitbags. The exit was made through a narrow bath-shaped aperture located towards the tail. The aircraft itself was never popular with the Company, although the quality of the flying and navigating of 38 Wing was far superior to that of the Americans who later flew us in the relative comfort of C.47s – the old Dakota, which as an aircraft was by far the easier from which to jump.

Parachuting for the first time in the heat of Africa was something of a novelty. The air was thinner and the fall faster than in Europe. Some lightweights, however, caught in an upward thermal current, actually found themselves rising rather than falling once the canopy opened. Tommy McMahon once hung in the air with no sign of ever coming down for several minutes after the stick with which he had jumped had hit the ground. The thermal finally released him and he floated down with a new record for the longest time taken over an 800-foot drop.

The best times for making a drop were early morning or late evening. During the day the hot winds, variously called 'siroccos' or 'khamsins' had an unpleasant way of springing up from nowhere and building up momentarily to gale force. To be caught in one of these whilst parachuting could have only one result. Some of the battalions suffered a number of casualties in this way. The company, prudent in its choice of jump times, had none. These dust storms or 'whirling dervishes' were quite a curse at Froha. So far as the Company's lines were concerned the situation was aggravated by their proximity to the airstrip.

Though the sand was rolled and dampened from time to time, it was little better than a levelled bit of desert. Every time an aircraft took off clouds of dust arose and were blown over the tents. Often enough the heat would cause these dust clouds to be whirled along like a great water-spout. Woe betide anything which lay in the path of these monsters, which towered hundreds of feet in the air: tents, papers and anything loose went sky high. If caught in one all one could do was curl up in a ball and cover as far as possible ears, eyes and nose against the penetrating grains of stinging sand. At meal times, no matter how well you might cover your mess tin the contents inevitably became coated with a fine film of grey-brown powder. Though you might carefully scrape this off with a spoon, the food yet retained a dusty taste and grit became part of the daily diet.

Flies were another great pest. No matter what sanitary precautions were taken flies were always around at meal times. Mosquitoes, too, plagued us at night though mosquito nets and anti-mosquito cream helped. One could never be quite sure a mosquito was not already inside the net when bedding down. The persistent high-pitched buzzing of a mosquito often had one slapping away in the dark hoping to hit the unseen target. The anti-mosquito cream caused one to sweat more profusely and many swore that it attracted rather than repelled the little pests. Nevertheless, it was advisable to use the cream if on duty outside. As soon as the sun began to sink (and it sank fast in these parts) it was 'longs on and sleeves down' to minimise the target area.

Our time at Froha was, happily, not long. It was already clear that the Division was preparing for an operation somewhere along the Mediterranean coast of Europe or on some nearby island. An island seemed the more likely target, initially at any rate. There was speculation about Corsica, Sardinia or Sicily. Others considered a landing in the South of France or even Italy. The glider pilots were also busy and the Company saw, for the first time, American Waco gliders, ugly looking things compared to the graceful if somewhat sinister black Horsas of the Glider Pilot Regiment.

The Company continued with a training programme of sorts. The heat tempered enthusiasm, but a route march in the cool of the early morning made a welcome change from the confines of the camp. Weapon training was a bore. Most of the men knew as much about small arms as their NCO's, who were hard put to it to hold the men's attention. Of most interest were the

map-reading sessions. The Company had been brought up on
the excellent English Ordnance maps. Now they had to get used
to reading foreign maps, mostly French and on a far smaller
scale. Adjustments had to be made to the distances involved.
The difference between kilometres and miles had to be assimi-
lated.

In the third week of June orders were received to entrain for
Tunisia. Most of the Company faced an uncomfortable week of
travel in cattle trucks through the none-too-interesting line-
of-rail country of Algeria into neighbouring Tunisia. A lucky
rear party, consisting of Lieutenant Spivey and Sergeant Kent's
section of 1 Platoon, cleaned up the camp and, after handing it
over on the day following the Company's departure, flew in
Dakotas to an airstrip near Kairouan and acted as advance party
to prepare for the rest of the Company's arrival.

A small olive grove on the south side of the Kairouan/Souse
road not far from the Arab village of M'Saken was allotted to
the Company. Apart from a marquee for stores and another for
the officers' mess and orderly room there were no tents. The
marquees had to be drawn from the depot down the road along
with other stores for the Company. Siting and erection of the
marquees, stacking away the stores, digging latrines and
drawing up platoon lines occupied the advance party in the days
that followed.

All through the long, hot, dry months of July and August and
the early days of September this was to be the Company's
home, improved where possible by the scrounging of the extra
tent, the odd piece of canvas and camouflage netting to form
another amenity however simple. Here the Company came to
know the cicadas, those shrill chirping tree-crickets, and the
ant-lion and the scorpions. The mosquitoes and the flies were
still with us, but perhaps the worst aspect of the conditions in
which we had to live was the lack of water.

We were rationed to an individual pint a day supplemented
some days by the twice-daily issue of cookhouse tea, ladled out
sparingly by CQMS Lax and Catering Corp Corporal Gordon.
The Company water-truck would go off each day to draw the
ration of water allotted to us. The queue among the olive trees
would form anything up to an hour before the truck's return,
usually late in the afternoon. On one occasion it did not return
until long after dark. It had broken down and took hours to get
going again.

From somewhere, by some means, the Company acquired a

collapsible, canvas-sided infantry assault boat used for section river crossings. It could hold ten men at a pinch and was just such a boat as would one day ferry some of the Company across the Lower Rhine. For the present it served another purpose. Placed beneath the largest and shadiest olive trees in the Company's lines, with its wooden struts in place, it was filled to a depth of six to eight inches with precious water from the water truck. It soon became the most popular gathering spot after parades were over for the day. Men bathed in it, scooping mess-tin after mess-tin of the tepid water over themselves. They also washed their small washing, socks, underpants, PT vests and shorts, in it. The water soon took on a distinctly brown muddy appearance as the red-brown sandy soil of the olive-grove found its way from the ground to the water by way of the men and their rinsed-out garments. The water was changed every couple of days but was always brought to the same colour and consistency within a matter of hours. No one minded that, however, and the boat remained the Company's private lido until the Company left for other parts.

The general monotony of life under the olives was relieved in many ways. Because of the heat, the CO turned night into day – in other words, the Company did an eight-hour day of training in the cooler hours between 20.00 hours and 04.00 hours. This chiefly involved route marches and map-reading exercises as well as physical training sessions to keep the Company from getting sluggish. Sleep between 04.00 hours and 07.00 hours was all right, but by 08.00 hours the Company would be bathing in its own sweat. Most felt compelled to get up and catch the liberty truck which ran almost daily to the sea at Souse, 20 or so kilometres away. There the Company could bathe and swim to its heart's content until midday, when the truck would transport the men back to camp and a meal for which they were more than ready.

Corporal Gordon, the Company cook, did his best with limited resources to vary the main meal of the day, which was served in the evening. Basically, he had only bully beef and Maconachie-canned stew to work with, but he did wonders with them. Bully beef fritters with sautéd onions (somehow procured locally), supplemented by re-constituted potatoes, a sauce of his own making and a substantial hunk of very good locally-produced bread was a popular menu. He sometimes made his own savoury biscuits. Local fruit, tangerines and oranges rounded off the meal. Prickly pears from the abundant cactus in the vicinity, as well as water melons purchased from the local Arabs, also formed part of the diet. The prickly pears were an acquired taste. The hairlike spikes which were part of their make-up made eating them something of a hazard. The prickly pears had a taste similar to the banana.

Crude games of handball were organised on an open field adjoining the olive grove. A sort of league was built up. Games between individual sections led to the selection of teams to represent each platoon. Platoons would then play off against each other. The result is lost to history. They were rough, tough games and one sergeant, at least, lost a front tooth as a result of an over-enthusiastic tackle!

The Company had its first active service casualty among the olive groves of M'Saken. 'Frenchy' Henderson sustained a nasty bite from a scorpion in his sleeping bag. His whole arm swelled up to twice its normal size and turned an ugly blue-black. It was thought he might lose the limb, but, happily, this cheerful, tough, swarthy Corsican was returned to the Company some time later, complete in all his parts.

In July the operations on Sicily, which are dealt with separately, led to a blot on the Company's escutcheon. A certain sergeant was found with a gunshot wound in his foot, which rendered further active service out of the question. He was supposed to have been cleaning his pistol when it went off accidentally. No one, least of all an experienced sergeant, cleans his pistol without first removing the magazine and clearing the action of the weapon to ensure there is no bullet in the breech. The Sergeant in question was an old hand, a regular soldier, who had seen active service in France and was evidently, now faced with it, not anxious to see any more. He was whipped off to hospital and never heard of in the Company again.

Though the story of the Company's part in the invasion of Sicily is told elsewhere, it is appropriate here to mention the loss of the Company Commander, Major John Lander on the night of July 13/14. He did not have to fly on the mission, but he was anxious to see how his men managed things. The Dakota he flew in was shot down off the coast of Sicily and he perished with it. Someone who knew him well, Lawrence Wright the author of *The Wooden Sword* talks of him as 'The Mad Major' and describes him as 'a splendid person destined to do great things, but in him perfect courage was combined with imperfect vision, and he flew with a confidence that observant passengers might not share.' Lawrence Wright has some delightful tales to tell of John Lander which are worth repeating and will surely not offend if repeated here. Here are some of them intended as a tribute to the man who laid the foundations of the Company.

'John Lander, the Mad Major, wore medal-ribbons of 1914-18, but he wore the new parachute badge too. He would take his young corporals on cross-country runs and wear them out; they devised the trick of giving him the lead while most of them dived into a haystack on the airfield boundary. An unlucky few, chosen by toss, still ran to give the semblance of a pack. As these few sweated home with the Major, the loafers would join up astern, but fresh as they were, and anxious to register their presence, they seldom passed the Major on the home stretch. He never went by car if there was time to walk. A "stroll" with him was an ordeal that one learned not to repeat. He played football with schoolboy zest: he played pushball at Ringway against huge Polish paratroops, and when the resulting shoulder dislocation was put right, he played again. When he thought he was unobserved he wore glasses, but never when flying with an instructor or a passenger. He achieved a remarkable cross-country flight in a Tiger, with a compass that he had failed to lock and was slowly rotating by vibration; a line joining the landmarks that he identified later proved to be a spiral. Yet I cannot recall that he ever broke anything. I only once saw John Lander nervous. That was the day he went home and had to let his mother first see his parachute badge.'

Lawrence Wright was here speaking of a period in the early training of glider pilots and John Lander wore the wings of a glider pilot as well as those of a parachutist. He was indeed squint eyed and near sighted. Writing of an early glider exercise, arranged for the benefit of visiting VIPs, in which Major Lander took part at Ringway, Wright recalls, after mentioning the performance of some of the other pilots: 'Lander, moreover, had demonstrated the permeability of a thickset hedge to a Hotspur-load of Army officers, when he took off as usual without his glasses, with his altimeter set a thousand feet too high. You could distinguish the Army from the Air Force observers at such exercises, apart from their uniforms, for when a loaded and brakeless Hotspur headed towards them, the soldiers would stand their ground in happy ignorance while the airmen unobtrusively drew aside.'

The loss of John Lander over Sicily was a great blow to the Company for he was held in affectionate esteem by all ranks.

'Boy' Wilson succeeded him as CO and on the morning our new commanding officer announced the death of our remarkable founder it was seen that he had inherited not only the badges of rank but also the anklets which his late superior officer had had specially made. It seemed a strange, unjust and ironic coincidence that the Company's very first fatality in its very first action should be its founding officer. This is especially tragic since John Lander was merely flying as an observer on this occasion and need not have gone, but being the man he was nothing would have stopped him going.

Major Wilson (as he now was) proved to be a most worthy successor and led the Company from then on with distinction. Lieutenant R. E. Spivey took his place as second in command and soon inherited 'Boy' Wilson's Captain's 'pips' just as the latter had inherited John Lander's major's crowns.

After the Sicily operation, life under the olives along the road to Kairouan went on much as before. On 1 August some of the Company, notably No. 1 Platoon, carried out a parachute exercise using Albemarles, at night putting out lights for a glider landing. A week later the Company had Dakotas of the US Transport Command allotted to it for the first time and another night drop was carried out. Navigation was not the strong point of this formation as experience in Sicily had shown and many of the Company landed far from the intended DZ. Four days later another parachute exercise was carried out using the same planes. There were two things which marked these exercises, the one concerned the issue of parachutes, the other the unwelcome experience which befell Sergeant Allerton.

A number of Italian prisoners of war had been allotted to the Company and did camp fatigues under CQMS Lax and Corporal Gordon. It was in keeping with the CQMS's sense of humour to have the Italians hand out the parachutes to the men about to use them. If they had been so minded it would have been the easiest thing in the world for the Italians to sabotage each 'chute simply by interfering with the 'ties' which formed a vital part of the opening mechanism. Fortunately, no such thing appears to have occurred to these cheerful prisoners, who were probably having a better time with the Company than they ever had with their own army.

Val Allerton, on one of these jumps from a Dakota, found himself caught up under the tail of the aircraft from which he had jumped. It is necessary for the pilot to fly these aircraft 'tail high' when dropping parachutists in order that this fouling of the tailwheel be avoided. Either the pilot had let the tail come too low during the drop or Val's parachute had malfunctioned. Whatever it was, it nearly cost him his life. He found that his helmeted head was being bashed against the underside of the Dakota's rear fuselage and all efforts from the inside of the 'plane to pull him in having apparently failed, he contemplated ending things himself by removing his helmet and allowing his head to be bashed in. Fortunately, he passed out before he could take this fatal step. The men inside the aircraft made superhuman efforts and after a long struggle succeeded in freeing him from the tailwheel and pulling him back along the fuselage to the door. After a further dangerous effort Val was dragged back into the aircraft. To test his nerve he jumped again a few days later.

Val's experience was not unknown: there had been incidents of this kind before. In one instance, all efforts to pull the unfortunate parachutist free having failed and the aircraft running short of fuel, the pilot headed out to sea. Flying low over the water and at near stalling speed, the static line was cut loose. The poor fellow fell into the sea and was drowned. The outcome of a similar incident, this time involving an old Whitley, had happier results. With great skill the pilot on this occasion made a front-wheel-only landing and as the Whitley lost ground speed gradually lowered the tail under which the man lay face uppermost. His parachute pack acted as a cushion and when the Whitley came to a halt at the end of the runway, he was able to get up and walk away with the tattered remains of his parachute hanging down behind, suffering from no more than shock.

This was one of the hazards which every static-line parachutist faced. The incorrect flying attitude of the aircraft or an improperly tied cord could result in the parachute failing to part company with the static line or in the parachute failing to open. Any of these possibilities would have almost certain fatal results. These things did not often happen, but often enough for everyone to be aware of them.

Life in Tunisia had its lighter side and the Company with innate enterprise and zest for life made the very best of it. There were almost daily visits to the sea at Souse for swimming or other recreation. Here, not far out, was a half-submerged wreck from which to dive into the clear sparkling water. From its deck fish and the occasional octopus could be seen wreathing its way along close to the sandy bottom. The wreck was later placed out of bounds after a chap from one of the battalions broke his neck diving too close to the sunken hulk.

A visit could be made to Kairouan, about 30 miles west of M'Saken, ranking as the third 'holy city' in the Moslem world. One visit was usually enough. This ancient walled city was exceptionally hot and had little to offer by way of diversion for western eyes. It was a city which teemed with Arabs and there were few Tunisian-French save civil servants. The huge mosque was impressive and formed the hub of the town from which narrow streets radiated like the spokes of a wheel. Each street was devoted to one particular trade or calling. There was a street of shoemakers; another for the weavers of rugs; a street of perfume mixers and sellers (a pleasant change from the pervading odour of camel dung); butchers' shops occupied another and there were eating houses of sorts and dark, dangerous-looking wine shops. Unhappily there was nothing approaching a decent pub in sight. There was, however, a long narrow alley, which attracted the curious and housed all the brothels in this holy city. The wares on sale were on view just as was the merchandise in all the other streets, but judging from what could be seen behind the barred, prison-like windows, the veiled females offered little attraction to the men of the Company, sex-starved though they were. For those who did venture inside the dark and smelly hovels there was a convenient prophylactic centre just outside the walls of the town. For those so inclined there was a better set of brothels in Souse where there were French girls or those who could pass for French. These had been inspected and passed 'FFI' (free from infection) by our own medical officers, but there were long queues for these amenities. Most of the men preferred to cool off in the sea rather than queue in the broiling sun. A very small percentage made use of the brothels and the absence of feminine companionship was seldom a problem and rarely raised in conversation. The Company lived strenuously and was preoccupied with soldiering and sport, food and drink. The latter was mostly tea, but there was a weekly beer issue. Officers and sergeants had the added privilege of an occasional bottle of whisky or gin at 7/6d a bottle for Booths or Johnny Walker!

One of the most memorable events which took place amid the olive groves of M'Saken was a concert party organised by the sergeants for the whole Company. To mark the occasion, the CO arranged for a huge barrel of local red wine – real rough stuff – to be on tap for all to partake of during the proceedings.

The stage was composed of full ammunition boxes covered with tarpaulin. A couple of stout poles and some wire draped with camouflage netting served as a proscenium. More netting strung on wires formed the wings. Lighting was arranged by the Signals Section. The programme was largely devised by Sergeant Joe Smith, who also wrote the lyrics of some of the songs as well as the script of a sketch described later.

The show started at 20.00 hours on a Saturday evening under the stars, with a day of rest ahead to look forward to. With brief intervals for the replenishment of mess tins at the wine barrel and with commendable continuity which would have done credit to a professional show, the show went on into the night. There was an astonishing amount of entertainment talent in the Company. The mood was set with the singing of songs well known to all parachutists. 'Jumping through the hole' and 'When the red light goes on', the latter sung to the tune of the 'Red River Valley', were two. A funny-man dialogue between two sergeants – one very small, the other very tall – based on actual humurous incidents in the Company's history and bearing veiled references to personalities well known in the Company, raised a lot of laughs. Then there was a contribution from Paddy Moore, his fine Irish tenor singing that bitter-sweet Irish song about 'the penny candle':

The English came to try and teach us their way . . .
And blamed us for being what we were
But they might as well have tried to catch a moonbeam
Or to light a penny candle from a star . . .

How Paddy could sing that song. Yet it was without bitterness or malice. He sang it on many occasions, in many places, and the Company loved him for it. A piano had been obtained from heaven knows where. It was out of tune but Sergeant George Seal somehow managed to get a tune out of it. So too did Joe Smith who sang his own compositions all about 'kitbags and glim lamps' (the Company's own special things) to the tune of the 'Blues in the Night'. It brought into the lyrics all the places we had known, and it must have been after Sicily because it mentioned the landing on the plains of Catania. Company cook, Corporal Gordon, showed himself a wizard not only in the culinary arts but with his conjuring tricks and illusions and earned the name which stayed with him 'The Great Gordini'.

A sketch, devised by Joe Smith, cast CSM Chris Keirnan as the hero, 'Handsome Harry' armed with pick helve coming to the rescue of 'Little Nell', played by knobbly-kneed Sergeant Waller of the Cameron Highlanders, from the machinations of the villain landlord, heavy black moustachioed, Joe Smith himself. The theme song for this sketch was 'Come to me my melon-cholic baby' – a reminder of the gripes some suffered from eating too much of the local water-melons. A display of unarmed combat between muscular blonde Frank Buck and Corporal Jack Schofield nearly resulted in Jack taking the count for good. No holds were barred and the 'falls' were for real – nothing faked.

The singing barbers – CSM Keirman and Sergeants Ron Kent, Joe Smith and Waller – gave their interpretation of 'Passadena' and 'Nelly Dean' and led the Cockneys in the singing of 'Any old Iron' and 'The Old Kent Road'. The Welsh, not to be outdone, sang 'Land of our Fathers' as only the Welsh can do it – Sergeants 'Nobby' Yates and 'Gremlin' Jones were the performers. Lieutenant D'Arifat from Mauritius sang 'Parlez moi d'amour' and for good measure threw in an impromptu tale of making love on the sandy shore of that exotic island.

Mess tins replenished at the wine barrel, the Company was in the mood to sing collectively. Sergeant Gordon Anderson was inspired to give his rendition of 'A Quaint Old Cornish Town'. This was soon followed by 'Old Uncle Tom Cobley and All' and a variety of other songs. The tone of the party began to deteriorate somewhat when the verses of 'The Good Ship Venus' and a recital of 'Eskimo Nell' took over and the officers, (reluctantly, one felt) left for their lines.

All in all, this concert probably did more to cement the spirit of the Company than anything before or since, until Arnhem. The latter was a long way off and many who were at M'Saken would not be at Arnhem. Equally, there were those at Arnhem who had not been at M'Saken, yet they inherited some of the *esprit de corps,* the foundations of which were laid in the olive groves of Tunisia, and soon of Italy.

The Company's near neighbours, in the olive grove just across the strip of tarred road, were Popski's Private Army. Not too much was seen of them, but the Company was very much aware of their presence. They had an unsettling habit of discharging a slab of gun-cotton each morning at the hour of their reveille. This might be at any hour between 02.00 hours and 06.00 hours. They were very well supplied with transport, mostly jeeps on which they mounted not only Brens but machine cannons from aircraft. After the early morning explosion, whilst the Company was trying to sleep, they would rev. up their engines and shortly after, roar off. They might not be seen or heard of again for days. The Company would always know when they returned. It was usually at dead of night. Another roar of racing engines, then silence would descend until the next blast of gun-cotton announced yet another reveille.

Popski's Private Army built themselves a first-class assault course amongst the trees and cactus on their side of the road. The CO prevailed upon them to let us use it on occasion. It had every kind of hazard ingenuity could devise (except water), from rope walks, tree climbs, ropes to swing across gaps, trenches to leap, wire under which to crawl and machine gun fire to squirm under. The first time it was used by the Company Popski's Private Army supplied the machine gun fire. It was too close for comfort. Thereafter we supplied our own!

Another diversion which some of the NCOs of the Company enjoyed was a two-day course in the use of what the instructor called 'hand guns'. The instructor was an American, Major Grant-Taylor. He came with the reputation of having been small-arms instructor to the FBI in America and to the Hong-Kong Police Force. He specialised in and taught the technique based on what he called 'the instinctive pointing sense'. As he was able very competently to demonstrate, it was a most effective way of transporting a bullet from the barrel of a pistol to the target. The technique also incorporated a defensive method of reducing the risk to the firer. 'The battle crouch' into which the pupil was taught to slide whilst engaging the target ensured that he himself presented the smallest possible target to any retaliatory fire. All this he first himself demonstrated. He was a real showman. Everything was set up and well organised to impress. With a brief 'Good Morning, gentlemen' he proceeded to draw a pair of pearl handled silver barrelled pistols and to put a neat hole straight through the aces of four playing cards at 20 paces distance. 'That, gentlemen', he said, 'is a circus trick. I am not here to teach you that. I am here to teach you – even the worst shot amongst you – how to survive in a close-quarter situation and to kill Germans.'

This he proceeded to do. Without weapons the pupils found themselves carrying out the movements of the battle crouch and swinging the arm and hand which would carry the gun up to point the index finger of that hand at any given target. Sufficiently practised in this technique, the real thing began with Colt. 45s and Browning 9 mm automatics. Snatching at the trigger as one came on to the target was negatived by the phrases 'Squeeze the pip out of the orange.' Most knew that the short-barrelled pistol or automatic tends to throw upwards at the moment of firing. Some of this was due to a tendency to jerk at the trigger, hence the admonition 'Point and squeeze'. Practice of the technique, with oil drums as targets, followed. When satisfied that his pupils were all capable of hitting them at 20 feet – no great accomplishment – he moved on to greater refinements. Firing on the move, as one threw oneself into the battle crouch, down on one knee or prone or even rolling over flat on the back.

His was a most instructive course even to those who already thought themselves experts in the use of small arms. It culminated in what Grant-Taylor called 'a practical exercise in the art of killing'. He had a Nissen hut rigged up to resemble a German Army office, with cardboard cut out figures representing the enemy. He entered by one door and exited by another and in the space of seconds emerged having placed a bullet in each of the targets. This he showed his interested pupils. Then he had the holes pasted up and the positions of the carboard figures altered. One by one each pupil went through the hut on his own to carry out the exercise Grant-Taylor had demonstrated. Major Grant-Taylor had much to say about the psychology to be employed in target selection and the art of spotting the most immediate source of danger.

The NCOs came back to the Company to impart these techniques to their men and phrases like 'the battle crouch', 'the instinctive pointing sense' and 'point and squeeze', and many others, became part of the everyday language. If it did nothing else this course inspired a greater confidence in oneself and in close-quarter weapons. Still, there were many who preferred the technique of tossing in a grenade before entering an occupied room or building. The rest might very well come in handy after that.

A visit to one of the most beautiful places to be found among the many on the Mediterranean coastline took the Company to the Gulf of Hammamet and the tiny village of Hammamet where there was a magnificent villa draped in bouganvillea and surrounded by lush-leaved palms. The villa was reputedly one of the resorts to which Edward, Prince of Wales and uncrowned king of England had romanced with Mrs. Simpson. A couple of days at leisure in this delightful spot was a welcome change from the dusty heat of M'Saken.

On one of the Company's night-into-day exercises, it had the use of a pair of Royal Marine DUKW landing craft and carried out its first and only sea assault landing. There was first the night march to the coast, then the setting up of platoon defence positions to meet the expected invasion from the sea. One platoon embarked in the DUKWs and put out to sea. At dawn after a short semi-circular sea trip, the landing craft nosed into the beach. A two-pronged attack inland from the shore brought the invaders into contact with the remainder of the Company's defence positions. After an exchange of dummy rifle fire and the throwing of 'thunder-flashes' the exercise ended and everyone went for a swim and a beach breakfast served by Corporal Gordon and his staff.

Soon after this a leave camp was set up for the Division near Nabeul, on the northern tip of the Gulf of Hammamet and marking the eastern extremity of the neck of the Cap Bon Peninsula, near Tunis. The camp itself was merely a series of tents drawn up in orderly lines above the high-water mark of the Gulf, but there was no other regimentation. Free to do what one wished – a day trip into Tunis – an excursion into the hills inland which had seen the last few days of the Afrika Korps in Africa; or merely to swim and sunbathe, read and in the cool of the evening visit the wine shops in Nabeul. Roll call was none too strict. All that the camp authorities required to know was whether you would be absent for any meals. Haversack rations could be drawn by those who planned a day out.

There are those of· the Company who can testify to the doubtful adventure of spending the night locked up in the Caspah (or Kasba), the walled Arab quarter within the sprawling city of Tunis. It was 'out of bounds' after curfew and visited from time to time by jeep patrols of Military Police. Dodging these and slipping out of the Caspah at first light and diving into the first available barber's shop next morning was quite an experience shared by Sergeants Kent, Philipson and Price. It had been a distinctly rough night in very mixed company.

The Company's time in Tunisia was running out. In Italy, Mussolini had resigned on 25 July and Marshal Badoglio had taken his place as head of the Italian government under the diminutive King Victor Emmanuel. The Sicilian campaign had closed on 17 August and as September approached the prospect of Italy dropping out of the war seemed imminent.

A visit from General Bernard Montgomery (as he was then), for which the Company lined the Souse-Kairouan road immediately in front of its lines in the olive grove, confirmed that the Division was now an integral part of the 8th Army for the campaign which lay ahead. A photograph facing page 120 of Hilary St. George Saunders' book *The Red Beret* records this occasion and many faces are easily recognised, among them Joe Smith, Slim Summerville, Bill Price, Bob Kendall, Captain Spivey and a number of others, the memory of whose names do not return as easily as do their features.

On 6 September the Company, along with the rest of the Division, received orders to move north to the port of Bizerta. As the trucks rolled along the dusty road through Menzel Bourguiba and beyond, they ran alongside airstrips on which Dakotas stood ready, and for a brief while it seemed that the Division might be delivered on Italian soil by air. With sleeping bags and kitbags and a full complement of arms and ammunition, the Company camped in the open on a rocky promontory not far from the seaport.

On the evening of 8 September General Dwight Eisenhower, whom most of the Division never saw in person, broadcast the news of the Italian capitulation, but still no positive orders reached the Company. It was quite evident that the Division was destined to land in Italy but the means by which it was to do so were not made apparent until the last minute. The Company went aboard the cruiser HMS *Orion*, which had taken part in the evacuation of British troops from Crete in 1941 and was lucky to survive repeated dive-bombing attacks and struggle back to Alexandria.

Once aboard the cruiser the Company learned that it was destined for the Italian port of Taranto, scene of an earlier aerial torpedo attack by the Fleet Air Arm. At the same time it was announced that 8th Army had already been launched across the Straits of Messina on to the toe of Italy. The Division was now to enter at the 'instep', secure the port and the 'heel' of Italy.

The Company had left its temporary home in the olive groves near M'Saken with mixed feelings. In spite of certain hardships it had been the scene of many good times as well as dramatic memories. Some of its number had left there for the Sicily operation on the eve of which the Divisional ammunition dump had blown up; most had returned there; others had not, notably our CO and founder, John Lander. It would always be remembered for that fact if nothing else. There was more to it than that, however. The first seeds of real comradeship and of *esprit de corps* had been sown there amid the sand, the cactus and the olives. The Company left that place a better, harder and more closely-knit unit, full of confidence in its own ability and ready and eager for whatever might lie ahead.

The Company would return briefly to Tunisia and again make the railway journey along the lowland flanked by the Atlas Mountains into Algeria later in the year, but for the present no thought of this possibility occurred to anyone.

It was at M'Saken that the Company received its full complement of officers, Lieutenants Grierson (1 Platoon), D'Arifat (2 Platoon) and Peter Baker (3 Platoon), as well as a few more recruits from England, amongst them Harold Sims, who had fought in the Spanish Civil War and had a medal to show for it.

4 SICILY
July 1943 – 'Chaos'

'Fustian', the overall codename given to airborne operations on Sicily, let it be said at once was a shambles. This was not the fault of the men of the 1st Airborne Division who, in spite of everything which went against them, gained their objectives. The reason for the shambles lies in the inadequate training and experience of the predominantly American aircrews flying the various missions. Added to this was the lack of communication between services which led to the Royal Navy opening fire on Allied aircraft.

Three distinct operations for the 1st Airborne were planned. On the night of the seaborne invasion the glider-borne 1st Airlanding Brigade consisting of only two battalions, the South Staffords and the Borders, were to land near Syracuse, seal off the port and seize and hold the bridge nearby until relieved by the seaborne troops of 8th Army. It was decided, much to their disappointment, that the 21st Independent Company would not be used, for fear of alerting the defences; this, in spite of the fact that the landings were to be made at night and the landing zones were anything but ideal. On a narrow neck of land bordered by sea-cliffs, rocky slopes and dense orchards the gliders were required to land in very small fields separated by stone walls without the aid of 'Eureka' and landing lights.

On the night following the initial landings the 2nd Parachute Brigade were expected to land near Augusta, some 20 miles further north. Again it was to be a night landing and the Company stood eagerly by to provide lights and the aid of

Eureka. On some later night, depending on the progress made by 8th Army, the 1st Parachute Brigade, led by Brigadier Gerald Lathbury, would land near Catania, north and south of the Simeto River to capture and secure the Primosole Bridge ready for the 8th Army's northward advance on Messina. At the same time American airborne would be landing to the west in advance of seaborne landings of their own troops to carry out a left hook in conjunction with the 8th Army's straight right and thus embrace the whole of the island. Such was the plan.

It was perhaps as well for the pathfinders that their services were not called upon at Syracuse and the Ponte Grande. They would have stood a good chance of being dropped in the sea, or at best in most unsuitable conditions on very rough terrain. The wind rose for one thing. The Navy's flak deterred some tug pilots for another. Gliders were cast off too early and some landed in the sea. Others were scattered over an area of 25 miles. Of the six Horsas ordered to land 'coup de main' beside the Ponte Grande, only two reached the correct area and one of these blew up on landing, killing all aboard. Three others landed two miles away and the troops they carried did eventually reach their destination.

The success of Operation 'Ladbrooke', as this initial effort was called, might have been enhanced if the pathfinders had been used, but as subsequent events were to show too much depended on the pilots flying the transports and they were proved not to be up to the task. By 06.30 hours only 87 of the battalion faced an Italian infantry battalion and held the objective against superior numbers for nine hours. At 15.30 hours, with only 15 men left unwounded, they were overrun. They had removed the demolition charges so that when the Royal Scots arrived, six hours late, the bridge was still intact and retaken without too much difficulty. The Brigade had taken 490 casualties and the glider pilots 88. These casualties might have been fewer and the whole operation more effective if the pathfinders had been used, but both this and what the pathfinders' own casualties might have been is in the realms of speculation. Given properly trained pilots the whole thing should have been a much cleaner proposition.

However, the seaborne follow up and the securing of the Ponte Grande did enable 8th Army to make such progress next day as to render the drop of the 2nd Parachute Brigade unnecessary. At the eleventh hour it was cancelled and those men of the Company detailed for the drop near Augusta who had drawn and fitted parachutes, gone to the airfield and actually emplaned, returned frustrated to the olive grove near M'Saken. There is hardly anything worse for morale than the let-down of a cancellation after this buoying up of courage in contemplation of that flight and jump into the unknown. It was something men of the Company were to experience many times before going to their final destiny.

The landings at Syracuse had taken place on the night of 9/10 July. The next phases of airborne operations had to await events and did not take place until three more days and nights had passed. Operation 'Marston', the third task allotted to the Division, was to be carried out by 1st Parachute Brigade. Its objective – the capture, intact, of the Primosole Bridge spanning the Simeto river rather less than ten miles south of Catania. On the morning of the 13th, Montgomery, in his caravan HQ some 20 miles south of the bridge, predicted 'I shall be in Catania tonight'. Across the Mediterranean, on airfields around Bizerta, the three fine battalions of 1st Brigade waited for the words which would send them into action. With them were a few select members of the Company. Back in the olive grove at M'Saken other members of the Company, some of whom still felt dejected because of the cancellation of 2nd Brigade's operation, waited for news of their comrades in this the Company's first operational task. Among the men who were to go to Sicily were Sergeants Seal and Smith, Corporals Stan Brown and Dick Wilkin, Privates Carter, Crighton, Gibson and Sharman.

Originally briefed for the night of 12 July, it was not until the evening of the 13th that the Brigade became airborne. Weather conditions had caused the operation to be postponed for twenty-four hours. Such postponements are commonplace in the life of the airborne solider, but could be trying, leaving each man to speculate whether the next twenty-four hours would see them on their way or result in the cancellation of the operation, as had happened in the case of 2nd Brigade. Once buoyed up to go, that was all the average man wanted to do.

The night of the 13th found Joe Smith in the same aircraft as the CO of 1st Battalion, the renowned Alistair Pearson who 'won four DSO's and a MC in eighteen months'. 'I was jumping No. 6 or 8 – with a bloody great kitbag of lights and batteries' Joe Smith writes, 'and Colonel Pearson was a couple of places behind me.' In a following Dakota, Stan Brown was jumping No. 1 in his stick and like Joe, he had 'a kitbag weighing about a hundred pounds strapped to my leg.' Unknown to either of them or for that matter anyone in the Brigade, other parachutists were heading for the dropping area but from quite another direction.

General Kurt Student had been agitating, ever since the invasion of Sicily had started, to fly his XI Corps in to counter-attack the Allied landings. As a result, the German High Command (OKW) released General Heidrich's 1st Parachute Division. On 12 July this formation started to move. The first waves of the German parachutists began landing on the plain south of Catania that afternoon and General Kesselring was there to watch them arrive. The German parachute operation continued on the days that followed.

These were the men who, along with the Schmalz Battle Group of the Hermann Goering Division and the Italian Napoli Division, would oppose the 1st Parachute Brigade and cause Montgomery's predictions to go wildly awry. Catania did not to fall to the 8th Army until 5 August.

Meantime, in the air, the 1st Brigade was experiencing some of the chaos which the Air Landing Brigade and the American airborne had suffered during their flights and landings. Long before the, predominantly Dakota, formations reached the dropping zones they were in difficulties.

Stan Brown's aircraft, flying a course which took them first over the small island of Pantelleria (captured only the month before), and then on to the western edge of Malta, before heading on a north-easterly course for Sicily itself, were given 'a pretty hot reception from Allied ack-ack gunners'; and again 'As we approached the island we were met with what appeared to me to be a solid wall of anti-aircraft fire.' Standing in the door waiting to jump Stan had, perhaps, the most awesome view of what he would have to leap into. 'The tracers formed the most remarkable display of fireworks I have ever seen. It seemed to me that it would be quite impossible to pass through. The pilot must have had similar thoughts because we did a violent bank and headed towards the sea. The performance was repeated many times over the next hour. I could hear the rattling of shrapnel on the fuselage and the 'stick' behind me were being thrown all over the 'plane.' Stan describes this experience as 'operational parachuting at its worst'. As other aircraft and gliders arrived to join the milling mass of troop-carrying aircraft, a number crashed in flames into the sea or on the shoreline.

Somewhere in the, by now quite formationless turmoil, Major Lander was flying as an observer. He had gone along (as we have seen) just to see how effective was the Company's pathfinding equipment. In Alistair Pearson's aircraft, Joe Smith in the body of the Dakota was seeing rather less than Stan Brown but none-the-less experiencing the same delay and violent flak-dodging tactics of the American pilot. The story is told in *Airborne to Battle* (Tugwell) that after observing that his aircraft was flying up and down the coast without attempting to fly inland, Pearson removed his parachute and went forward to the aircrew compartment, where he found a young navigator who had completely lost his nerve. Patting his pistol holster meaningly Pearson is reported to have said, 'The bloody man ought to be shot'. He ordered the pilot to change course and fly in over the island. Pearson had just got back to his seat and locked on his parachute harness when the jump light came on. The 'plane dived steeply as the men made their exits and in the result there was hardly sufficient height to permit the tailenders' parachutes to develop fully before they hit the ground. Joe Smith's account of the drop bears this out.

'The comic opera of the Yank's flight discipline,' Joe says, 'doesn't now bear recall. Alistair P. did unhook when we were overdue, went forward, came back and hooked up again. On the next run-in we did get the red and the green, the latter coming miles too early. The stick had to be held back by 1 Para's I.O. (who was jumping No. 1) until we were over the road. There was no attempt to throttle back and on exit my kitbag was literally torn from my leg.'

In the exit door of his Dakota, Stan Brown was already reflecting that any hope of laying out the landing lights and operating Eureka successfully was gone – 'we were way out of time'. The 'planes he and Joe should have been guiding in were already there and 'I was still airborne.' But not for much longer for suddenly 'our pilot more in desperation than anything else, went right in: the light came on and out I went. The sky was alive with tracer. I appeared to be sliding down a path of coloured lights towards the ground which to my horror was a blazing mass. Luck was with me. I landed just on the edge of this holocaust. Another parachutist landed almost on top of me.'

When Joe Smith jumped and parted sudden company with his kitbag his first instinct was to grab the rope to check the fall of the bag. He did so with an ungloved hand and sustained a nasty rope burn across the palm. In the few seconds he had to assess the situation on the ground he realised that he was dropping into fire. 'It was like Dante's Inferno. The wheat fields were burning and it was a matter of luck not to drop into a burning area.'

Once on the ground both Joe and Stan (though they were not to meet on the ground until daylight) turned their minds to the job in hand. Stan Brown enlisted the aid of the man who had landed beside him to lug his heavy bag off the DZ. 'By some miracle, I found myself on the river bank and had a fair idea of where I was. I knew we were about one and a half hours late and parachutists and gliders were coming down everywhere. I decided it would be ludicrous to attempt to put out a flare path as the whole DZ was ablaze.'

Joe Smith on the other hand, who probably landed quite a bit earlier than Stan, decided to do what he could with what he had. He put out his lights and found that the signal light for morsing the recognition sign was broken. He improvised by turning the light bulb in its socket. All to no avail, he considered, since he figured that no one could pick out the glim lamps in all that fire and smoke. Still he did it. For over an hour he persisted with his manipulation of the light bulb. He considered that as there was some moon, the bridge, the river and the high features of Johnny I and II to the south of the river would be adequate land marks for any glider pilot worth his salt who reached the area. Joe had no Eureka with him as this would only be of use to the leading aircraft of a formation equipped with Rebecca and not to a glider pilot. After hearing a couple of 'whooshing' sounds overhead announcing the arrival of gliders Joe packed up and made for the bridge nearby. Here he found some of the 1st Battalion and one of the German paratroops (now a very upset prisoner and wanting to die in battle) and settled in a slit trench to await the dawn.

On the river bank Stan Brown joined the hundred or so men of the 1st Battalion who had congregated there. Among them was Alistair Pearson who, when the numbers reached near 200, sent one party off to attack the garrison of Italians who were supposed to be guarding the bridge. The rest were sent to hold the bridge which had been captured intact from the north by about 50 men of 1st Battalion led by Captain Rann at 02.30 hours, on the morning of 14 July. The confusion of that night is hard to put into words: each individual would have his own personal account of it.

There was, for example, the man in the 3rd Battalion, dropped north of the bridge out on the Catania Plain who was approached in the dark by a dimly seen figure who asked, in German, 'Have you seen my Schmeisser?' With a muffled 'Nein' the British paratrooper put as much distance as he could between himself and his questioner, and joined his comrades.

North of the river, Sergeant Seal and Jock Crichton had landed and done what they could to bring in 3rd Battalion successfully. Then they too made for the bridge after destroying their Eureka in the prescribed manner.

Only four of the gliders Joe Smith was supposed to bring in near the southern end of the bridge landed intact; nine others either crashed on landing or were lost at sea. One of the gliders which reached the right area just failed to clear the river bank, landed badly, broke its back and dumped its rear half in the river in a welter of men and equipment. The pilots were badly cut about, having been thrown through the perspex window of the cockpit. The survivors crawled out of the mess ashen-faced. Any parachutist seeing this would say 'Thank God I go into battle by parachute and not by glider.'

When dawn came 1st Brigade were in possession of the bridge from which the demolition charges had been removed. About one third of 2nd Battalion were on Johnny I, guarding the bridge from the south, under Lt. Col. Johnny Frost.

With the dawn came the inevitable expectation of counter-attack. Stan Brown helped to lay some Hawkins mines across the approach road to the bridge. These came in handy that morning. At dawn on 14 July there were about 250 men of the Brigade in the immediate defence of the bridge. At 08.00 hours, after the leading scout car of a German convoy had reaped the benefit of the Hawkins mines, and 'everyone fired at anything' in Stan Brown's words, he and Joe Smith linked up for the first time since they had left North Africa. Stan Brown recalls: 'After that episode, I glanced along the span of the bridge and there, as though on a school hike, was Joe Smith. Was I glad to see him!' Joe says: 'I made my way over the bridge to 1 Brigade HQ; where I met Stan Brown.'

They shared a slit trench during the time in which, as Joe Smith recalls, 'There was considerable shelling and air bursts.' And Stan Brown says: 'A FW 190 dived on us; doing its best to see that we never rejoined the Company!' Joe, who had lost his Sten gun, now sported an Italian carbine with an attached bayonet. Stan Brown, having looted the wrecked scout car, says: 'It's a strange fact that the enemy's weapons always appear more attractive than your own.' At some stage during the morning Stan lost the heel of his boot. He thinks it was during the aerial attack. He recalls that there was plenty of mortaring going on at this time. Casualties at the bridge were mounting.

The slit trench which Joe and Stan occupied was alongside the river to the west of the bridge and the pillboxes which guarded it on the south side of the river. As the heat of the morning became more unbearable they moved into the shade of a nearby Horsa's wing. There they scraped a fresh weapon slit in the hard-baked Sicilian soil.

The first enemy reaction to the Brigade's presence on and around the bridge was an aerial attack. Messerschmitts, firing cannon and machine guns, flew over at low level but caused little damage. An attack was then put in by a body of German paratroops who had been dropped south of the river. This attack, which was supported by mortar fire, was unexpected since it was considered that the defenders' main strength lay in the garrison at Catania to the north. The attack was repulsed with difficulty. The mortar fire was kept up, intermittently, all day.

Brigadier Lathbury was briefly in wireless touch with 8th Army at about 09.30 hours and it was learned that 4th Armoured Brigade was meeting stiff resistance out of Lentini, but that it was driving north as hard as it could. More counter-attacks were delivered as the long, hot, day wore on. It could only be a question of time before the holders of the bridge were overrun. They were too lightly armed and what ammunition they had would soon be expended.

Only three of the eight light anti-tank guns had arrived and were in position to deal with tank attacks from the north. Two 3-inch mortars made up the only other available 'heavy' armament. These, too, were low in ammunition. A little way south of the bridge, 16 Parachute Field Ambulance had set up a Casualty Clearing Station where in impossible conditions (including visits by German patrols) 72 operations were performed on the wounded. Late in the afternoon, a German 88mm gun began shelling the pillboxes until they became untenable.

There was no indication of the presence of Colonel Johnny Frost's 2nd Battalion on Johnny I and II, but it was to these features that Brigadier Lathbury decided the surviving defenders should withdraw that evening. No such orders reached Joe and Stan in their hole under the glider's wing. However, detecting something was taking place, Stan crawled to neighbouring slit trenches only to find them empty! Deciding it was time to move, he and Joe together crawled along the ditch which brought them to the all-but wrecked pillbox where someone – possibly Captain

Gammon who had been blasted from it – told them to join the
rear elements now making for Johnny I.

Back along the ditch and into an orange grove they went.
Here Stan decided that he could no longer resist the urgent call
of nature. While Joe stood 'rear' guard, he very decently went
behind a tree and lowered his trousers. At this juncture the last
of the Brigade came pounding through the trees saying that Jerry
was hot on their heels. There was nothing for it but to join the
retreat at top speed with Stan holding his carbine and small pack
in one hand and his disarranged trousers in the other.

They made good their way up the slopes held by 2nd Battalion
which was then of rather less than company strength. Being well
behind the main body in the fading light they came in for some
unpleasant sniping from their comrades on the hill before
reaching the summit. Here, Stan Brown says quite prosaically,
'A light snack and tea was provided by someone. We were
allotted positions in the defence perimeter.'

It has never failed to astonish enemy and ally alike, how the
British soldier, even in the oddest of situations, will always,
somehow, contrive to have a brew of tea! The traditional
'brew-up' in moments of crisis must surely have been one of the
key factors in the British Army's morale throughout the war. It
was a factor in British civilian morale as well, from which it was
inherited. No commander of any unit, right down the line to
platoon and section, could afford to ignore it. A brew of hot tea
somehow restored a sense of proportion, as if to say, 'Well, if
we can manage to make tea in all this, things can't be too bad,
can they?'

After the heat of the day, the men on Johnny I settled down
to pass a cold but quiet night. At first light the expected relief
put in an appearance. 'It was during my period of sentry duty
that I heard someone approaching my position,' says Stan
Brown. 'I challenged and received the welcome reply. "Durham
Light Infantry".'

That morning, 15 July, they watched, from the comparative
safety and height of Johnny I, an attack put in by the DLI
supported by the forward elements of 4th Armoured Brigade. It
failed to take the bridge. 'They got an almighty hiding,' Joe
Smith writes. The bridge remained in German hands all that
day, but they failed to destroy it before being driven off during
the night of 15/16 July. The demolition charges were safely on
the river bottom and they had no others.

On the 16th the survivors of 1st Parachute Brigade descended to the road to be transported south to Syracuse where sea transports waited to take them back to North Africa, their job done. Together Joe and Stan walked down the slopes to the road and looking back once they were on the road, saw a large sign marking the field they had just crossed. 'Minen' they read. They had just crossed unscathed, through a German minefield!

At Syracuse, Joe and Stan somehow were parted. No doubt Joe's restless energy sent him on the prowl, for he says he met George Seal whom he had not seen throughout the action. Together with Jock Crichton, all four arrived back at Sousse and from there to M'Saken, where they were welcomed by the rest of the Company. There they learned of the death of Major Lander, shot down over Sicily; that Nick Carter (of the ginger hair) and his pal, Hank Gibson, had flown on the operation but had not dropped; and that Alan Sharman was missing, his fate unknown.

And so the Company's first operation had come to an end. It cannot be said to have been an unqualified success. It had failed to accomplish the high aims set for it by its founder who had himself lost his life. This was no fault of the men, who had individually had their courage tested and not found wanting. The mission on which they had been sent should not have been a difficult one and was well within their capabilities, if only the air side had been better managed. The expenditure of valuable, expensively trained airborne troops by transporting them in aircraft manned by raw aircrews, inadequate in the field of navigation and incapable of dealing with battle conditions, was the responsibility of higher command.

So far as the pathfinders were concerned, one lesson had been learned. They would in future only fly into action with equally well trained *pathfinder* aircrews, who could be relied upon to deliver them ahead of the main body on time and on target.

It is appropriate here to speculate on how those fires on the DZs were started. The German pathfinder technique – if such it can be called – for night operations was much less sophisticated than that devised by Major Lander. They simply had pathfinder aircraft fly into the drop area, shortly before the troop-carrying aircraft, and there lay two lines of incendiary bombs; one just short of the DZ; the other just beyond. The Germans then baled out between the two resulting lines of fire. As the Germans were operating on the same night and in the same area as 1st Parachute Brigade it is probable that they started the fires.

The German technique lacked the precision which would later mark the British D Day landings and those at Arnhem and across the Rhine, which enabled individual units to be brought down on predetermined spots and so facilitated the forming up of those units on the ground. By contrast German airborne operations were inevitably scattered, unco-ordinated and confused, as a study of their Crete landings will show.

The story of the Company's part in the Sicily campaign would not be complete without recording what befell Dick Wilkin and Alan Sharman. They had been assigned a rather different task to that of the others. It was not for them to bring in a mass drop of parachutists nor yet a squadron of gliders. Instead, they were to fly in a single aircraft (an Albemarle) with a detachment of commandos, some of whom had not jumped before. The idea was for Dick and Alan to show them how it was done. They would drop first and, with Alan operating a Eureka set carried in a kitbag, bring the commandos down on a suitable dropping zone.

The objective was a small bridge across a deep gorge through which the River Salso flowed. This bridge was to be destroyed, thus severing an important internal link in enemy communications and so hampering the switch of troops and guns from one coastal flank to the other. The objective was near the small town of Nicosia, slightly north and east of the centre of Sicily and not to be confused with the larger town of that name on Cyprus.

It was the sort of job which a section of the Company might very well have carried out successfully. Just why unfledged commandos should have been chosen for the job when there were experienced parachutists within the Division available, is a mystery. The drop area would inevitably be hazardous, for it lay in the Monti Nebrodi range of mountains which runs on a north by north-east diagonal between the peaks of Monti Zimmara (4374 feet) on the west and Monti Soro (6060 feet) to the east.

On the night of the first Allied landings, the Albemarle carrying Dick and Alan encountered some flak as it crossed the coast but, being the RAF, the crew carried on inland unperturbed. At about 00.30 hours, Dick and Alan moved into position near the exit aperture and prepared themselves for the jump. It was a bright moonlight night and they could see the tops of the barren mountains resembling a lunar landscape far below them.

The two pathfinders had asked for a ten second 'red' warning light before the green signalled them to jump. Suddenly, to their astonishment, the green light came on without any red. They were far too high, but after only a momentary pause in which they queried this turn of events across the open space, it was mutually decided that they should jump and out they bunny-hopped.

At that height (about 5000 feet) the drop was long and the resultant variable drift spread 'the stick' which followed them out, over a wide area. Alan Sharman had time to see the rest of the stick drifting away behind a mountain ridge and into a neighbouring valley. He realised that he would be quite alone on landing. The extra weight of his kitbag with the Eureka and other gear he carried gave him a more direct descent and less drift. The mountainside on which he landed effectively cut him off from his comrades, whom he never saw again, with the exception of Dick Wilkin, but that was much later.

There now began for Alan Sharman a long period of exposure, hardship and danger to which a lesser spirit might well have succumbed. His first instinct, after coping with a difficult and heavy landing on the rocky hillside, was to bury (rather than destroy) the Eureka set. It might yet come in handy. In all probability it still lies crammed in the deep rock fissure which Alan found for it!

Having effectively hidden the set, he scrambled down a hillside path which led into a narrow, cultivated and obviously populated valley. His arrival provoked the loud barking of dogs and he soon decided that if he was to avoid capture he would have to get back high on the mountain. The approach of an elderly peasant, who ran off when he saw Alan's drawn Colt pistol, convinced him. So for the next hour or two he climbed back uphill and finally curled up under a bush to rest and wait for daylight.

At dawn he peered out of his bushy hideout and with the aid of his escape map endeavoured to get his bearings. A few miles up the valley he could see a small village clinging to the hillside. He identified this as (probably) Capizzi, ten or twelve miles from Nicosia and a place to be avoided. The country was very wild and rugged and after much thought he dismissed any idea of linking up with the men who had dropped in the next valley. They had either carried out their task by now or been captured.

He decided to lie up by day and move easterly and southerly by night. In this way he might link up with the advance of 8th Army. For three or four days he moved in this fashion, drinking what water he could find from infrequent streams, eating locust beans and what grain and grapes he came across in the night, but resolutely hanging on to his emergency ration. Miles behind enemy lines as he was, he did not consider that this was an emergency!

Barking dogs giving his position away were his greatest hazard and one night he discovered that he was being actively sought by an Italian patrol. Strung out in line they were advancing towards where he lay in thick brush. He drew and cocked his pistol ready to shoot his way out but hoping he would not have to. He heard the Italians shouting to one another. He was probably right – they were trying to keep their own spirits up and hoped they would not encounter the dreaded 'paracutisti'.

They had not seen him. This was obvious, for one Italian, who came within a pace or two of where he lay before seeing the cocked Colt pointing at him, turned and ran away, yelling at the top of his voice. Sharman took the opportunity of the diversion the shouting Italian created to put as much distance as he could between himself and the patrol. No effort was made to pursue him – a typically Italian reaction. They were probably too busy listening to their comrade's account of his confrontation and disbelieving it.

Holed up once more for a lonely cold night, Alan welcomed the rising warmth of the sun and awoke one morning to find that he was overlooking a busy main road, with truck loads of Germans and military traffic passing all day long below him. He found it strange but fascinating.

By the fourth or fifth night he was feeling distinctly groggy from lack of food and exposure. He took a desperate chance and visited a valley farm where, with two gold Napoleons from his escape kit, he bought from an old woman, a great bowl of pasta, a loaf of bread and a lump of Parmesan cheese. He retired with his feast to his mountain cave. It was not long before he received a visitor: a villainous-looking, black-bearded Sicilian armed with a shot gun. He may have been of friendly intention, but it is more than probable he was out to collect a German reward for captured parachutists. One look at Sharman's pistol pointing at his head was enough to deter him, however, and like the previous two encounters it ended with the retreat of the Sicilian. Alan, too, decided it was time to move on.

That day he heard the sound of gunfire far to the south – it could be the 8th Army approaching Catania. For the first time – a little light-headed – he decided to move to the sound of the guns (as all good soldiers do) – by daylight. It was a mistake. As he rounded a bend in the mountain track he ran slap into an Italian patrol. To his surprise he was allowed to pass. He was not wearing his red beret and he thought and hoped he might pass as a German. The NCO was, however, suspicious and called after him in Italian. As casually as he could, Sharman replied 'Tedesci' and almost at once realised his mistake. He had used the Italian derogatory term for the Germans – a word no German would use concerning himself. He found himself covered by the whole patrol and realised that he was a prisoner.

That night he lay in the gaol at Nicosia. By a strange coincidence, he found under the leg of a rickety table a small wad of paper. On it were the names of the commando captain and some of the men who had jumped with him from the Albemarle! Dick Wilkin's name was not on the list; he was presumably still at large.

From Nicosia, Alan was moved to Capizzi under a German escort in a Volkswagen and from there to Messina after twice being strafed by the RAF and taking cover in the roadside ditches. At Messina he joined a mixed bag of airmen, paratroops and infantry POWs and was under heavy guard in a large house. Next day they were some of the first Allied troops to land in Italy. They were taken to Gioia Tauro and were due the following day to entrain for the north and ultimately, Germany. Alan Sharman had other ideas about his destiny.

He reconnoitred the station yard in which the prisoners were confined, seeking an avenue of escape. He found himself teaming up with an officer named Bridgeman-Evans, an able-bodied seaman named Mason and a German-speaking Jew who went by the name of Wells. Together, after watching and timing the movement of sentries, they made good their escape over the wall and into the street below, utilising a convenient tree.

Once outside they mingled with Afrika Korps troops in the streets of Gioia Tauro, with Wells chatting away loudly in German as they passed the street-side bistros. The Germans did not even give them a second glance. Outside the small town, going south, they took to the cliffs to avoid the busy road, heavy with German traffic.

The night was spent in a ruined hut overlooking a beautiful little bay in which a dozen or so fishing boats bobbed at anchor on the gentle Mediterranean. Very tempting those boats looked.

An early reconnaissance told them that there were Italian sentries posted at 100 yard intervals and that a Breda machine gun covered the beach.

That night as soon as the moon went down the four escapees crept down the hillside to the beach and at a point between two sentries began the painful inch by inch crawl down to the water's edge. Somehow they reached a boat undetected and found it heavy and hard to handle. Mason, the seaman and Wells somehow got aboard and Captain Bridgeman-Evans took the tiller. Sharman was still in the water keeping the boat head on into the sea and was last to climb aboard. Just as a clear escape seemed possible the noise of clambering over the side of the boat finally alerted the sentries. There was the sound of running feet and a challenge. The occupants of the boat tried to get it moving. Though dimly lit the bulk of the boat was a sufficient target and the sentries opened fire at close range. The Breda MG joined in and soon the boat was holed. Wells was wounded by a large splinter of wood and Sharman took a bullet through the right armpit and shoulder. Bridgeman-Evans and Wells went over board to give up, at least for the time being. Bridgeman-Evans would later escape again from Strasbourg into neutral Switzerland. Wells would be killed trying to escape again. The boat was sinking fast and Sharman could do no more than hang on with his good arm. Mason probably saved his life by pulling him back into the boat, which was now half submerged. Then he too swam ashore. Sharman was alone in the sinking boat. He took another bullet through the top of his right thigh.

Somehow he was brought ashore and carried on a stretcher to the cliff top. At Mileto near Vibo Valencia he was operated upon without anaesthetic by an Italian surgeon who evidently did a good job and was decent enough to give him a glass of Cognac and a cigarette.

After seven weeks at Mileto, Alan Sharman, aided by the Italian surgeon and his own fitness and constitution, found himself on the mend and able to walk. The surgeon told him that the 8th Army had landed in Calabria and was advancing northwards. Vibo Valencia was bombed and there was some shelling in the area by a monitor anchored off shore. The hospital was left untouched.

Soon after this Germans arrived to arrange the evacuation of German wounded and prisoners of war. Left unguarded for a short time, Sharman slipped down to the basement kitchen run by Franciscan nuns from Sardinia who hid him in a cellar store.

The cellar had a small ground-level fanlight through which he could watch what went on outside.

For the next two days, ever fearful of detection, he saw the retreat of the Germans. Tanks, half tracks and infantry passed his look out. At the end of two days, with the passing of what he thought was the last of the German withdrawal, Sharman decided to venture out and move slowly south. His first contact with 8th Army was with two forward scouts of the Cameronians carrying Bren guns. Soon he was amongst the flying column of Jocks marching to the skirl of bagpipes.

Before long Alan Sharman, having been twice wounded and twice escaped, rejoined the Company – a splendid example of the type of soldier to be found within its ranks. Very few knew of what he had been through and it is only after many years that the author has been privileged to learn the whole story.

Sicily finally fell to the Allies and was cleared of Germans on 16 August when, much to his annoyance, American units entered Messina ahead of commando units of Montgomery's 8th Army.

5 ITALY
'The Great Swan'

The Company embarked at Bizerta on 11 September and within 24 hours arrived in the harbour at Taranto as light was failing. It was still light enough to see huge Portuguese men o' war wallowing in the oily calm water at the harbour mouth. Earlier in the day elements of the Italian navy were sighted on the way to their surrender at Malta. This and the prospect of seeing a new country was interesting and exciting. We were witnessing and taking part in a little bit of history.

Tragedy marked the landing. The fast minelaying HMS *Abdiel* carrying the Company's old neighbours of Larkhill days, the 6th (Royal Welch) Parachute Battalion, struck a mine as she entered the harbour. This in turn detonated mines carried by HMS *Abdiel*. In the result the ship was blown in half and the 6th Battalion lost its CO, Lieutenant Colonel Goodwin (who had taken over from Pritchard who now commanded 2nd Parachute Brigade), a major, two captains, three subalterns, its RSM and 51 other ranks. In addition, four officers and about 150 men were injured. This was a grievous blow. In war, death and disaster can strike from anywhere. Here were men, ready to risk their lives on the opening of a parachute in face of enemy ground fire, meeting their fate in a manner least expected of airborne troops and in circumstances about which they could do nothing.

The Company's own landing was uneventful. Transport was the immediate problem. There was none. Around midnight the Company marched out of Taranto and took up positions on its outskirts. When dawn came it was to find that there was an

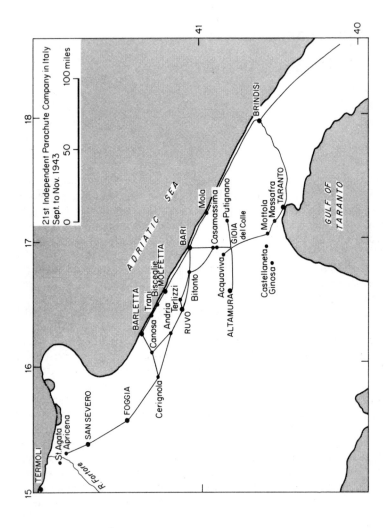

21st Independent Parachute Company in Italy
Sept. to Nov. 1943

Italian MG post sited just across a small ravine. This was quickly and peacefully seized just in case the fellows manning it were still of a Fascist frame of mind. They were not. It appeared that the Germans were pulling back everywhere before 8th Army on the west could cut them off. Italians, where they were encountered, were intent on surrender and getting out of the war.

Patrols were the order of the day. Probing patrols, just to see how far back the enemy was going before making a stand. Transport was captured, commandeered, serviced and put to work. The Company jeeps arrived and with Bren guns mounted fore and aft leading a commandeered truck, a patrol of platoon strength left for a two-day sally to Bari and back without incident.

Local patrols were also carried out on a more or less *ad hoc* basis. Within a few days the Company moved up the road to Gioia del Colle where there was an airfield and where the day before 156 Parachute Battalion had had a bit of a fight with the German rearguard. Their Major Pott won an MC and Private Sowden an MM there. The Company passed through the small towns (little more than villages) of Massafra and Mottola. En route, small jeep patrols dipped into Ginosa and Palagiano. It was quite possible to encounter the retreating Germans in any of these places since they too sent back patrols and would sometimes fight small delaying actions.

The Company's stay at Gioia del Colle was brief, but the opportunity was taken by many to pay a call at the 'Casa Rouge', quite a superior brothel, far better run and serviced than any encountered in North Africa. The girls were quite wholesome, the Madame strict but fair. If the service was rather brisk it was also very reasonable at 15 lira. The British occupation lira was worth 400 to the pound sterling at that time. Solace at the 'Casa Rouge' could be had for the equivalent of nine pence! But everything is relative, after all. A parachutist, officer and man alike, risked his neck every time he jumped for the princely sum of only two shillings a day, a rate of pay which never changed throughout the war.

What did change was the Madame's prices. When the Company revisited Gioia del Colle only three months later the price had risen to 300 lira. We talk about inflation! There in Italy in 1943 the price of this particular commodity had increased by 2000%! The Americans were blamed, although in fact there were only a few aircrews and ground personel stationed at the nearby airfield.

Out of Gioia, the Company probed further north. Jeep patrols visited Altamura, Acquaviva, Putignano and Casamassima. On only one of these was serious opposition encountered and the Company sustained its first casualty in Italy. One of its Jewish members was badly wounded by machine-gun fire. The rest of the Division was also making its forward probes and news reached the Company from time to time of brisk actions taking place on its flank.

It was at Castellaneta that the Divisional Commander, Major General 'Hoppy' Hopkinson was killed when, too eager to see what his men were doing, he was shot through the head by a burst of machine-gun fire. His place was taken by Major General Down CBE, who continued to command the Division throughout its stay in Italy.

There came a day when it was evident that the Germans had decided to pull back in earnest. The company was ordered forward a considerable distance. With trucks, Italian and German, captured and put into serviceable condition, the Company was rushed forward in a probe towards the considerable airfield at Foggia.

On 19 September the 4th Parachute Brigade returned to Taranto, its place having been taken by the 1st Air Landing Brigade. It was as a spearhead for the latter that the Company now proceeded on a north-westerly inland route running parallel with the Italian east coast through the small towns of Bitonto, Ruvo and Andria. From the main axis of advance light patrols in jeeps probed east and west along the way. The weather was fine and incidents few. Each village 'liberated' organised its own welcoming celebration. If the villagers appeared en masse it was a sure sign the Germans had pulled out. If, on the contrary, it was quiet with hardly a civilian in sight then the Germans were not far away. German patrols were engaged in much the same fashion – putting out patrols in the area they had just vacated to see how far the opposition had reached – keeping in touch with our advance. As a patrol of the Company motored cautiously into a village, a German patrol was, not infrequently, motoring out. Occasionally the simultaneous arrival of each side at opposite ends of the village would surprise them and shots would be exchanged. A pitched battle seldom ensued – but that was not the objective of either side.

In all this advance the Company suffered no more casualties, other than one which was due, not to enemy action, but to the instability of the old model Sten. Sid Humphries sustained a nasty nick below the knee cap when his section sergeant, rounding some rocks, accidentally caught the toe of his boot against the butt of a Sten leaning against a stone and pointing straight at where Sid was busy cooking for the section. The miserable weapon fired a 9 millimetre bullet at Sid's leg. Sid's reaction was quite calm. He just stood there looking surprised and amazed at his sergeant as if to say 'I'm not that bad a cook, am I?' Some speedy first aid from 'Doc' Toms and a day or two's rest of the leg and a few more days of stiff leggedness and Sid was back in action again.

After a number of days, advancing by leaps and bounds, there came an evening when the Company found itself lying under the guns of the 1st Air Landing Brigade just short of Canosa, about 140 miles, as the crow flies, from Taranto. The Company was in the inevitable olive grove a few hundred yards ahead of the guns awaiting the evening meal when it came under shell fire for the first time during the advance.

It is not clear who started it, but the Company was left in no doubt that it was lying under counter-battery fire for which no thanks were rendered to the gunners of either side. As suddenly as summer lightning, shells began to crack overhead both incoming and outgoing. From the rear came the heavy detonations of our own guns whilst overhead the Company collected a number of airbursts. Slivers of shattered steel rained down among the olives. The Company clung close to the tree trunks and began to dig some sort of meagre shelter in the soft earth among the roots. The shelling went on for some time, but as darkness fell the shelling eased and ceased altogether as the Company queued to receive the first hot meal it had had in days. The Company realised that the shelling was not meant for it.

Before first light next morning the Company was ready to mount the assembled trucks and move off up the road through Cerignola. The objective, and that of the Air Landing Brigade, was to test the defences of the major airfield at Foggia. It was a stop-start business as the forward elements of the Brigade ran into opposition along the road and on the flanks. Various elements of the Brigade set about the task of clearing this opposition. When it was done the Company moved forward again until another rearguard post was met.

Occasionally, when shelling or mortar fire was directed straight down the road at the Company transport, the men would dismount and take up positions in the ditches on either side of the road, whilst the transport moved back, out of harm's way, until the opposition either withdrew or was overcome.

At the end of the first day, after leaving Canosa, the Company was within a few miles of Foggia where it was expected there would be stiff resistance. Some days before, the Allied airforce had gone in and made a thorough job of neutralising the town itself and its rail-head. It had also 'had a go' at the airfield installations, but not so as to render it unusable by our own aircraft once the ground had been secured.

According to the Memoirs of Field Marshal Earl Alexander, 'the key airfields of Foggia were vacated by the enemy on 27 September.' Accepting this date as correct, the Company on the night of the 25 September lay under the guns near Canosa. On the following night it was just short of Foggia and east of the open road, which was entirely devoid of cover and in places was embanked. The Company, with its sleeping bags brought up by truck, bedded down in an olive grove just off the road.

Before it settled down for the night there was an incident which demonstrated the strain and tension of the past 14 days in Italy. 'Jock' McKnight, a normally quiet fellow, began to imagine Germans behind every tree and in every shadow. He ran amok and fired off his Sten gun in all directions to the discomfort of his companions. No amount of persuasion or pacification could satisfy him that the Company was not under attack. So he had to be overcome and given an injection of morphia. He was then sent off to the RAP and from thence to the General Hospital at Barletta. He was not seen again and the Company never did learn his ultimate fate.

There is reason to believe that he escaped from hospital and was killed on the railway line where, some time later, a decapitated and unidentifiable body in paratroop uniform was found. Ken Philipson, McKnight's close friend, made considerable enquiries about him, both on his return to Barletta and when he got back to England after the war and visited McKnight's home address. He was unable to find any evidence that his friend had ever returned to England and believes that the body found on the railway line outside Barletta was McKnight's. No other paratroops were in the area at the time and if it had been one of the Air Landing Brigade it is likely Ken would have heard.

On the morning of 27 September at first light the Company again took to the road north, but quickly came under mortar, machine-gun and a little later, artillery fire. Again the Company took to the ditches which, at this point on the road, were at the bottom of steep embankments. Here it was held up for some hours before receiving orders to fan out to the west and approach the Foggia airfield from the south and west.

No. 1 Platoon under Lieutenant Grierson was to act as the pivot of the Company's advance whilst Company HQ and the other two platoons were to move out to start points from small villages out on the plain. No. 1 Platoon would only move toward the airfield once a green Verey light from Company HQ indicated that the Company was in position for the advance.

After what seemed a long time to those waiting inactive, but which was probably no more than 30 or 40 strenuous minutes to the platoons moving into place on the plain, the green light soared into the sky to the west and the advance began. Soon sporadic firing could be heard in the west, but No. 1 Platoon, strung out in line, continued its advance right up to the airfield perimeter. It passed vacant parking bays and was soon approaching the hangars and other buildings skirting the airfield. Here and there was some evidence of bombing, some buildings shattered and still smouldering. Here, too, was the odd aircraft still on its dispersal pad but disabled.

Each building was approached with caution, each section putting down a Bren or riflemen to cover the advance of the rest of the section as it went from bound to bound, from cover to cover. A section, about to make an assault on a block of buildings, heard the sound of an engine racing and suddenly there burst into view a few hundred yards away a lorry filled with Germans (probably the last of Luftwaffe ground crews). It was quickly engaged by the section's Bren, but the target was not in sight for more than a few seconds as it raced westward and disappeared behind a belt of trees.

After this there were only occasional shots from the west as the other platoons advanced, and soon all was quiet. It seemed that the last Germans had left Foggia airfield. After clearing all buildings on and around the airfield the Company made its way, section by section and platoon by platoon, back to the road, the main axis of advance. As darkness fell the Company, together again after a hot, dry and strenuous day, marched back down the road to rest for the night in the shelter of a tank laager.

These were the first tanks seen by the Company during its advance. Unknown to the Company, the 78th ('Chopper') Division, which included the 4th Armoured Brigade, had landed at Bari, 60 odd miles down the coast, on 23 September. The tanks were the leading squadrons of 4th Armoured Brigade.

When morning came many realised how soundly they had slept. Some of the tanks had already moved off and the sound of their going had been missed by the heavy sleepers.

Again the Company assembled to move, this time into Foggia itself. The trucks were preceded by a couple of jeeps of the Company with Bren guns mounted and (most reassuring) a pair of tanks. On the outskirts of the town the Company dismounted and went forward on foot, 1 Platoon leading and section by section on alternate sides of the road, well strung out in single file.

As the main square was approached, with evidence on all sides of the recent bombing, a sniper became active from somewhere high on a building. He immediately drew fire from the Company's leading Brens and was not heard from again. The presence of a tank in the square with its turret manoeuvring menacingly must have also been discouraging.

The Company moved right into the town, each platoon taking an allotted sector to clear. There were warnings to look out for booby traps, but none was encountered. After entering a number of bomb-damaged buildings the Company was withdrawn. Neither Germans nor civilians had been met. Foggia was a ghost town.

From somewhere a camera still containing film was found and the writer has in his possession a faded sepia print of a photograph taken in the town that day. In the background is a bomb-damaged building and a telephone pole lying at a drunken angle. In the foreground, Sergeant Anderson and his section comprising Tommy McMahon, Johnny Melford, Paddy Cockings, Ken Philipson (with Bren) and Bill Dawkins, all grinning cheerfully, are looking distinctly warlike in battle order and wearing their berets at a jaunty angle.

The capture and fall of Foggia was something of an anti-climax. The stiff opposition expected had not presented itself. The Company pushed on again next day, another 30 miles or so. The weather, which had been good up to this point ever since the landing at Taranto, was beginning to break up. There had been a little rain the night before to lay the dust as the Company passed through Foggia and out on to the road which led to San Severo.

The Company had started out rather late in the day and now, as it paused on the outskirts of San Severo, night came quickly, with heavy black rain clouds building up for a storm. Very soon it was pitch dark night. The only light from the town below came from the red and yellow glow of a fire burning in what appeared to be one of the town's main buildings. Suddenly, the father and mother of an electrical storm broke immediately overhead, turning the scene below to one reminiscent of the old 'Dracula' and 'Frankenstein' horror films.

The town was seen for the first time with its buildings in sinister silhouette, with each vivid flash of forked and dancing blue-white lightning. The heavens opened and the rain came down in a deluge. The Company descended the hill and entered the town, in this dramatic setting. The main square with its imposing Town Hall was located and civilians began to appear.

It was soon learned that the Germans had only vacated the town that day after setting fire to the local granary which served as a depot for the surrounding farming area. They had also cut off the town's water supply. There were hard times ahead for this already impoverished district.

With the Company's arrival the whole town came to life; torches, reminding one of medieval days, lit the streets, carried high in the wind. In the Town Hall, candles lit the scene, and soon the Company commander was in conversation with the Mayor through Lieutenant Grierson, who could speak Italian. It was decided that each platoon would mount road blocks at the three entrances to the town. Billets for those not on duty on the road blocks were found with the aid of guides supplied by the Mayor. For the first time since leaving England the Company slept in houses that night.

During the next 24 hours reconnaissance patrols went out short distances, whilst those not manning the road blocks or on patrol were able to make closer contact with the local San Severans. There was the inevitable character who seemed to turn up in every town and village, the returned migrant from America. He was an inveterate scrounger, usually making it clear in his Italian Americanese that it was our cigarettes he was after. He invariably addressed one as 'Joe'. As in other places the old familiar phrases were heard again: '*Tedesci niente buono – Inglese buono*' and '*Benito finito*', which had a nice Italian ring to it. The '*tedesci*' were the Germans, who were no good. The English (now Italy was out of the war) were, of course, 'good'. There were also those in the jostling crowd who were all for denouncing local Fascists and seemed to think the Company should arrest them. The Company had other things to do.

The CO's reconnaissance in the area of Apricena a few miles north east of San Severo prompted the sending of No. 1 Platoon to Apricena next day, from whence a patrol under Lieutenant Grierson and Sergeant Kent and his section was sent out across the Fortore River. There was open plain beyond the river. The rest of the platoon waited in Apricena. They would keep the patrol under observation from the upper floor of an imposing villa perched high above the river. If the patrol ran into serious trouble a red Verey light would immediately bring reinforcements. The object of the patrol was merely to make contact with the enemy and by drawing fire, ascertain in what strength they might be; it was not intended to engage the enemy, but to return once the enemy presence and strength had been determined.

The patrol spent most of the morning crossing the plain beyond the river which had to be forded. It was a ten-man patrol which included Barney Moore with the two-inch mortar, Danny Gillespie with the Bren, Johnny MacManus, Paddy Gamble, Jimmy Cameron and three others whose names are lost to this writer. A call at a farm house about a mile out on the plain and the questioning of a pair of farm workers encountered en route led the patrol towards the higher ground on the far side of the valley.

The map showed a likely enemy stronghold in the shape of a monastery on the higher ground. Hidden from view by a belt of trees it bore the name 'Santa Agata'. This then became the patrol's objective. A good covered line of approach along a dry stream bed or 'wadi', with bushes and scrub offering cover from view, led the patrol up on to the higher ground on which Santa Agata stood.

Once on the high ground the patrol swung in line to face east towards the monastery just short of the westerly tip of the line of trees which had been masking the building from the south. The patrol was well strung out and about to begin its approach to the now sinister-looking building which had a high surrounding wall above which a line of small upper storey windows frowned down on the line of advancing men at a distance of about two hundred yards.

There was a sudden movement on the right front of the patrol and the fleeing figure of a man in the tropical gear of the Afrika Korps was seen haring along the edge of the belt of trees towards the monastery: a lookout, no doubt surprised by the sudden appearance of the patrol. Almost in the same moment as someone opened fire on the running target, MG fire opened up on the patrol from the windows of the monastery. The patrol went to ground.

Lieutenant Grierson, badly shot through the thigh, went down also. The Bren engaged the windows, putting short bursts into each of them in turn. There were a number of windows and it could not be seen from which ones the enemy fire was coming. There were certainly several guns firing – some might have been Schmeissers – but at least one was the unmistakable Spandau. There was barely any cover for the patrol on the flat open plateau on to which it had climbed. Sergeant Kent called on the mortar for smoke to cover the patrol's withdrawal.

The first bomb fired was HE, which burst against the wall of the monastery and gave the range. Smoke was successfully put down and those who could began to crawl back still under heavy fire from the building less than 200 yards away. The Bren gave covering fire as long as magazines held out, then it too withdrew in short bounds covered by Sergeant Kent, who in turn moved back whilst the Bren fired its remaining magazine in short bursts. Mustering the men who had got back to cover below the crest of the high ground and with the belt of trees obliquely masking them from the monastery, Sergeant Kent counted heads. Lieutenant Grierson and two others were missing. Wounded or killed it had to be assumed.

After 15 minutes of calling to indicate a rallying point, a decision had to be made: whether to go back on to the plateau to look for the missing or to get back to Apricena without incurring further casualties. Lieutenant Grierson had put up a red Verey light shortly after the patrol came under fire. It could be assumed that the rest of 1 Platoon would be on its way. Remembering that orders were to merely contact the enemy and establish their position and strength, Sergeant Kent reluctantly decided to withdraw by the covered route which the on-coming reinforcements would almost certainly take.

Half way back to the farm on the plain and still in the cover of the wadi, contact was first made with Sergeant Anderson's section. With him was the CO, to whom Sergeant Kent reported what he knew of the position and his guess that Lieutenant Grierson and probably two others were casualties. The platoon moved on.

Soon further firing broke out on the plateau and during the afternoon the Company's old neighbours, Popski's Private Army appeared on the scene with jeeps and brought the wounded Lieutenant Grierson out and with him Barney Moore who had remained with him and the other missing member of the patrol. At the villa in Apricena it was obvious that

Lieutenant Grierson's wounds would take him out of action for a long time and he was lost to the Company.

Apricena and the monastery of Santa Agata marked the northern-most point of penetration of the Company in Italy. By now the 78th Division and 4th Armoured Brigade were moving up to take over from the much lighter armed Airborne. The Loyals Regiment with a couple of its armoured cars had put in a late appearance at Apricena. It was logical that expensively trained airborne troops should be withdrawn from front-line activity as soon as possible. They could be held in readiness for surprise action behind enemy lines.

The Company had covered something over 300 miles into Italy in the space of about three weeks. The going had been relatively easy, but now the Germans were about to establish a firm line in the hills and mountains across the narrow leg of Italy before winter set in. No. 1 Platoon's patrol had reached, on the east coast, almost the same parallel of latitude as that on which Rome stood. Yet it would not be until 4 June the following year that the Allies entered Rome itself. There would be many long and bloody battles inbetween.

The Company moved back to Barletta, where it manned road blocks for some days but generally had an easy time, visiting the town and swimming in the Adriatic Sea. It was now well into October and still by no means certain whether or how the Airborne Division would be used in Italy. Then came a long march south through Canosa, Andria, Corato and Ruvo (where time out was taken to help the Italians tread grapes for wine-making), then on through Terlizzi and Bitonto, until finally the Company was housed in the outbuildings of an imposing farm with a fine old stone mansion of a house, part of which housed Company HQ.

Most of the several days' march took place in pouring rain. Transport was so short that during each day's march only a platoon at a time could be transported a short distance. The rest would march on until it caught up with the transport and then it would be the turn of the leading platoon to ride the next leg and the platoon which had had its ride would fall in in the rear and carry on marching. In this leapfrog fashion the Company covered 60 or 70 miles until it reached the farm between Bitonto and Bari, with each platoon marching about two-thirds of this distance and riding the remaining third.

A comparatively easy time followed, with no special duties and merely a little light training. A Company sports day was organised and enjoyed by most, but we had little equipment for team games. Still, it was pleasant to take rambles in the surrounding countryside without having to be constantly on the alert for the enemy. October gave way to November and more rain.

On 16 November the Company were allotted some Dakota aircraft and a parachute drop was arranged to take place at night somewhere near a bridge inland. The American pilots were supposed to find the DZ by following the briefing: 'You will fly to the coast and over Bari you will turn left and fly up the coast. When you come to the third river mouth turn left and fly 30 miles inland. That's your dropping point. Take off at 22.30 hours. Drop at 23.05 hours.'

Previous experience of American hit-or-miss flying led most stick commanders to stand in the door and follow the route with the aid of a torch, anxiously checking each land mark against the map. Fortunately it was a bright moonlight night and when it came to counting rivers at least one stick commander was able to tell his despatcher 'You're up the wrong creek' and although the red light was on 'You can tell the pilot I'm not going to jump unless he turns this kite around, finds the coast and the next river.' The despatcher disappeared to consult the pilot.

The red light went out without changing to green. The men had all stood up on the red and were pressing hard against the stick commander in the door. When the red went out it was as much as he could do to resist the automatic impulse to jump, but he did. The aircraft made a tight turn, found the coast and eventually the right river. The stick arrived half an hour late. 'Where the hell have you been?' the CO wanted to know. 'I had a pilot who couldn't count up to three, sir', the stick commander replied. That little exercise over, the Company, which had been transported to the airfield at Gioia del Colle for the purpose, returned to its rural existence on the farm.

Soon after this the Company was moved still further south and received a visit from Major General Down. It was learned that the Division would be returning to England via North Africa. Aircraft were in short supply so the journey would be made by sea. Troopships also were in short supply so the Division would be going first to North Africa until a ship could be made available. Finally, 2nd Brigade would remain in Italy as an airborne strike force for 8th Army and one of our platoons would be attached to act as its pathfinders.

This news naturally caused quite a buzz within the Company.

Which platoon would be chosen to stay? Just how this was decided was not known. Was it drawn from a hat? Was it left to some platoon commander to volunteer? Or was it a straightforward decision by the CO? Probably the last. The platoon chosen was Peter Baker's No. 3 Platoon. No. 1 Platoon was without a platoon commander, although it had probably the most experienced men and NCO's; No. 2 Platoon was good and had an excellent platoon sergeant, but Lieutenant D'Arifat was junior to Peter Baker, who was the obvious choice for this independent command.

As it was, Lieutenant D'Arifat as well as Peter Baker, who became Captain, remained behind to serve with No. 3 Platoon, which became the 1st Independent Parachute Platoon of the 2nd Independent Parachute Brigade. When the time came for the rest of the Company to depart there were farewells to be said to old comrades like 'Gremlin' Jones and his name-sake 'Gus', Sergeants Yates and Pickering, 'Dutch' Holland, Bowditch, 'Jungle' Medlicott, 'Ginger' Patton to name but some.

The Company left Italy by troopship for Taranto to Bizerta that much the poorer. It had not fared badly during its brief spell of action on the Continent but it had lost Lieutenant Grierson, as well as McKnight, missing believed killed, and another badly wounded in one of those early patrols. It was also once more without any platoon officers. The Company depended a great deal on its sergeants, who were of a very high calibre, as would later be shown, for no fewer than six were to attain commissioned rank, and five were to win Military Medals.

The return to North Africa can be told briefly. From Bizerta the Company went by rail on a week-long journey in cattle trucks to a tented camp just outside Blida in Algeria. It endured the winter rains, which were torrential and washed out tent pegs and collapsed tents and marquees. Some sergeants had a week of hospitality with a tank regiment and learnt to drive Sherman tanks and to fire their 75 mm. guns. A Company scaling of the nearby heights of the Atlas mountains and such like diversions filled in the time until, on Christmas Eve, a troopship became available at Algiers to transport the men back to England. It poured with rain as the Company stood in its ranks, waiting under arc lights on the docks of Algiers to board the troopship. It looked to be anything but a happy Christmas. Once aboard, however, a splendid Christmas dinner was laid on and when the ship put to sea on Christmas Day the Company's spirits rose at the prospect of the home leave awaiting them in England.

1. W/O Keirnan and Sergeants of the Company, Italy, 1943. (*Standing l. to r.*): Sgts. Gordon (ACC), Marks (RC of S), Binick, Brown, Carter (REME); *seated*: Sgts. Wilkins, Taylor (RAMC), Kent, W/O Keirnan, Anderson, Yates, Smith; *foreground*: Sgts. 'Gremlin' Jones and Pickering.

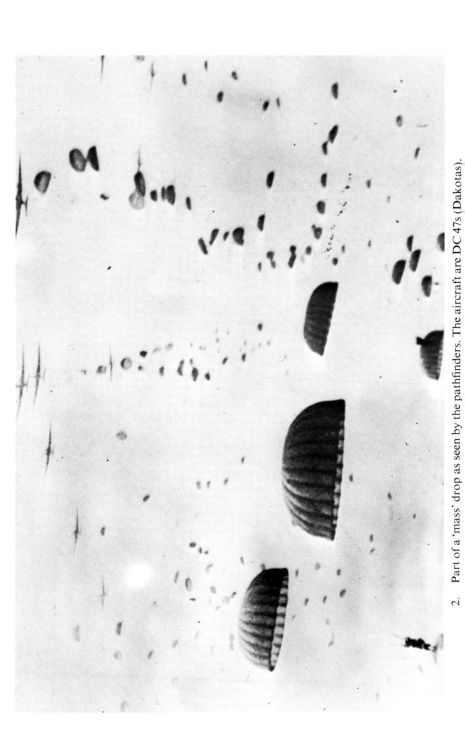

2.   Part of a 'mass' drop as seen by the pathfinders. The aircraft are DC 47s (Dakotas).

3.   Major (later Lt. Col.) B.A. Wilson in the centre of a group of Polish officers after briefing for Operation 'Market'. *Left* (with shoulder harness) Captain R. E. Spivey.

4.   A 'stick' of No. 3 Platoon before take-off, Fairford, 1944. Sgt. Thompson centre. Stirling bomber in background.

5. No. 1 Platoon of the Company, Italy, 1943 (after action at Apricena). *Back row (l. to r.):* Pte. Gordon, Barney Moore, Tommy MaMahon, Paddy Gamble, Heath, Hobbs, Coupland, not identified, 'Smokey' London; *second row:* Ginger Bell, Cpl. Schofield, McArthur, Bruce (I), Melford, 'Tex' Taylor, Sid Humphries,

Gillespie, Hewitt, Bruce (II); *seated:* Van Ryssell, Cpl. Cockings,
Sgts. Kent, Binick, Smith, Anderson, Travis, Bill Dawkins, (Absent:
Lt. Grierson—wounded); *on the ground:* McManus, 'Candy'
Marsland, Fenton, Joe May, Cameron, Phil Eden.

6. Sgt. Jim Travis (drinking—left hand in plaster) on DZ 'X', shortly after landing of 1st Parachute Brigade, Renkum Heath, 17 September 1944. With civilians and two of 1st Brigade.

7. Men of 9 SS Panzer Division approached our positions in Oosterbeek with caution—and rightly so. Arnhem, 1944.

8. One of the Parachute Battalion's heavy (Vickers) MGs in action.

9. Typical Bren gun position. Oosterbeek, 1944.

10. Supply drop over Oosterbeek, 1944. Note four engines indicating Stirling aircraft. The peaceful domestic foreground is typical of the Dutch landscape into which war came with unseemly violence.

6 ENGLAND
1944 – January to September
'The Waiting Time'

The Company's return to England was marked by 14 days' disembarkation leave, whereafter Lincolnshire became its new stamping ground. There were many adjustments to be made. Replacements were received to fill the gaps left by those who remained in Italy and the few casualties the Company had sustained. There were other people to replace also.

The Company had returned to England without a single platoon officer. Lieutenant Grierson had been badly wounded and the other officers, except for Major Wilson and Captain Spivey, had remained with the Independent Platoon in Italy. CSM Keirnan and Sergeant Gordon Anderson, along with Bill Dawkins, were selected for OCTU and officer status. Sergeant George Seal had earlier gone the same way.

A whole new No. 3 Platoon had to be constituted. We gained three new platoon commanders in Lieutenants David Eastwood (1 Platoon), Speller (2 Platoon) and Hugh Ashmore (3 Platoon) and CSM Jimmy Stewart replaced Chris Keirnan, who incidentally went on to become a Lieutenant-Colonel. CQMS Lax gave way to the younger 'Jock' McClellan who, unlike his predecessor, had completed a parachute course.

With the losses the Company had had and the necessity for reorganisation there were promotions in a good many directions. Sergeant Joe Smith became 3 Platoon sergeant and quickly established a close working relationship with Hugh Ashmore. Sergeants Binick and Allerton remained Platoon sergeants of 1 and 2 Platoons respectively. These three enjoyed a warm friendship which has endured over the years, though three more diverse characters would be hard to find.

The nucleus of experienced sergeants who remained were distributed amongst the three platoons as section commanders, supplemented by newly promoted NCOs who had proved their worth overseas; some staying with the men they had always led, others moved to 3 Platoon. The replacements were evenly distributed among the three platoons so that each platoon had a firm core of experience to train the newcomers to the ways of the Company.

The changes were made only after careful consideration and consultation among the sergeants who made the recommendations for promotions and took into account standing friendships and, avoiding the disturbance of section Bren and mortar teams, ensured that each Platoon had men experienced in the pathfinder role, signallers and Eureka operators. In training and practice every man could readily turn his hand to any of these things, but it was better to have men who specialised in these roles.

All in all the new intake was absorbed with the minimum of fuss; they quickly became fully integrated and were made 'members of the family'. Some of the very young went in awe of the 'veterans' who had already seen active service overseas. This was particularly so in the case of the senior NCO's who, to their young eyes, appeared older and more hard-baked than they really were. Many of these sergeants were still in their early twenties, but they had three years, or more war service and overseas experience behind them, and so it is not surprising that the 18- and 19-year-olds, with only a year's or at the most 18 months' service in England and fresh from parachute training, should have looked up to them.

There was, not unnaturally, a certain amount of 'line-shooting' about their exploits on the part of the men who had been overseas with the Company. Some of the replacements became a little tired of having their own inexperience held up to this exposure. One of them, 'Ginger' Alf Jones, played it down with a ditty, sung to the tune of an old music hall song 'One of England's broken dolls'. It went, in part, something like this:

> I was walking down the street the other day
> When a girl came up to me and she did say
> 'Why don't you wear khaki or Navy blue
> Like the other boys do?'

I looked at her and tears came to my eyes
And I said 'Lady, you don't realise,
When duty called I didn't tarry
I was fighting there at Bari
I'm one of Spivey's broken dolls
You shouldn't call me a dodger
I lost my balls at Foggia.

Other stanzas were added as events proceeded.

There were many others, of course, but not all can be repeated here. Clearly, in Ginger Jones the Company had acquired another character. There were many like him, but in their own way different. On the basis that if you cannot beat them, join them, some, like Private 'Umbriago' Hillier, who was later to prove his guts and character, emulated all the traits of the seasoned veteran. He earned the reputation of being 'a canteen cowboy' and a 'tailboard Romeo', always chatting up the girls at the NAAFI canteen and ogling and whistling at girls from the back of the Company transport. These were but two of the replacements the Company received. They soon became an integral part of this conglomerate of individualists, who none-the-less formed a formidable team under the fatherly leadership of Major Bob Wilson and there was never any real animosity within the Company. Instead, there was a friendly and healthy rivalry among the three platoons.

Each platoon liked to think it was the best and could do things just that little bit better than either of the others. In point of fact, when the chips were down, there was little to choose between them. In a subtle way, each platoon seemed to gain something of the character of the men who led them.

No. 1 Platoon was characterised by an air of steady, unruffled efficiency and utter dependability. It could have stemmed from the rather studious and unflappable platoon commander and the tall dignity of its platoon sergeant, who had all the poise of the ballroom dancing champion that he was.

No. 2 Platoon reflected the tough devil-may-care attitude of its platoon sergeant and something of the fire-eating potential which its platoon commander brought with him from the Battle School where, for a time, he had been an instructor.

No. 3 Platoon were 'the young ones', an impression gained from its youthful Hugh Ashmore, who in civilian life had been an actor, and from the black-moustached Joe Smith, the youngest of the three platoon sergeants, with his wide, white-toothed grin and sparkling dark eyes.

Over this diverse and, at times, wilful collection of individual characters there presided the paternal figure of Major Bob Wilson, a slightly built but incredibly tough and wiry figure who was far older than any officer or man in the Company. He had been born in 1900, yet when the Company parachuted, he parachuted; when it marched, he marched; when it came to recreation, he could hold his drink better than any and could enjoy a relaxed good time as well as the next man. Yet he carried the burden of command and cared for every one of his men as he would for a son. He was a fine judge of character and would not tolerate any one in his Company who did not measure up to his standards, but he was fair-minded and deeply understanding of human nature. He earned not only the respect but the affection of the men who served under him.

'CO's Orders', that time-honoured expression for the trial of military misdemeanours or breaches of discipline, were a rarity in the Company. Amongst men who were double volunteers and more often than not, treble volunteers, such proceedings were unnecessary. Most had volunteered for the Army in the first place and not waited to be 'called-up', next they had volunteered to parachute (as all parachutists did), and finally, they had volunteered to serve with the specialist pathfinder Company and had been through the selection process. In other words, every man was where he himself had chosen to be – with the 21st Independent Parachute Company – and was happy to be there.

It was hardly necessary, therefore, to impose the rigid discipline and 'Bull' associated with more conventional military formations. There was in consequence a fair measure of self-discipline, and if a few liked to wear their red berets at a somewhat more rakish angle than regulation called for, it was little more than a show of individualism, easily checked on parade by a firm word from an NCO.

The Company was essentially functional and operative. It was not given to ceremony, ceremonial guards and such like performances. When occasion required it, they could be as smart as any unit. Self-pride ensured a smart turn out, especially for walking out. Church parades, when there were any, were a voluntary affair, though jobs were always to be found for those who chose not to go.

In Newark Barracks the coal fatigue was a favourite chore on these occasions. Coal was needed not only for Sergeant Gordon's cookhouse but also for the hot water supply to the showers and ablution blocks. Some came to enjoy the coal fatigue. The cookhouse was always hospitable and provided tea and a foretaste of Sergeant Gordon's cooking.

With this background it is interesting to review some of the operations which were planned for the Division but which never came off. In April the Company made a drop in Rutlandshire and brought in a Brigade of parachutists at dawn. Two weeks later, a Divisional exercise called Exercise 'Mush' was carried out near Cirencester and some of the Company saw for the first time a mass drop in which parachutes became entangled and a man, with a kitbag attached to his leg, had a Roman candle and struggled to release his kitbag, only to land and receive the barrel of the Bren under his chin and thrust up through his head. The parachute settled on him like a shroud. Other men were scattered over the roof tops of Oakham and casualties were more than the planners could have contemplated.

In May the Company made another drop and brought in gliders. The Company travelled south for this and flew from their old airfield at Netheravon on Salisbury Plain. To some of the originals it was like coming home. These exercises led the Company to believe it might be used in the D Day landings which were obviously imminent.

It came as a disappointment when the Company learned that they had been passed over and that the initial landings of 6 June had been made at night by their sister company of the 6th Airborne Division. Some thought that it was due to the fact that on the return from Italy a new Divisional Commander had been appointed and one who had had no experience of airborne operations. General Down was, in the words of his successor, 'saturated in airborne experience'. He had commanded the 1st Parachute Battalion, the 2nd Parachute Brigade and in Italy, the 1st Airborne Division in succession to 'Hoppy' Hopkinson. Now he was assigned to the Far East to raise an Indian airborne division.

Major General Roy Urquhart came from the 51st Highland Division and was at first not well received. He was not 'one of us' and he felt this. Soon after his appointment he visited the Company. His burly, heavily-built figure impressed. He looked like a good 'bloke' in a scrap, but he was too big and heavy to make a parachutist. He would add considerably to the load of any glider. His testing time was yet to come. The Division reserved judgment.

It was, of course, logical that the 6th Airborne Division

should carry out the D Day landings for they had been formed and trained for that very purpose whilst 1st Airborne had been having their baptisms of fire in North Africa, Sicily and Italy. Even so, there was a sense of resentment that the senior Division had been relegated to the 'strategic reserve'. This was aggravated by the succession of 'on – off' operations which followed D Day.

The first of the many operations which engaged the Company's attention and energy was a plan (worked out before D Day) to drop the 4th Parachute Brigade on the D Day beaches in case the US 82nd Airborne Division encountered heavier opposition than was expected in the Cotentin Peninsula. This was, within days, enlarged to involve the whole of the 1st Airborne Division in a drop on the western side of the Peninsula near St. Saveur. By the march of events both these operations fell away as the Normandy lodgment took a firm hold. There was no need for the pathfinders' services nor for the employment of the Division in that area.

The planners turned their attention elsewhere. This time the British sector around Caen appeared on the maps in the briefing rooms and tents. Operation 'Wild Oats' would have taken the Company into a veritable hornets' nest in and around Evrecy and the airfield south of Caen. It was intended to assist the Canadian Division's break-out of the deadlocked position in that sector of the Allied front. It was called off just in time. Aerial reconnaissance discovered heavy flak batteries around the intended dropping zones and German reserves were concentrated in strength in the Evrecy area. The pathfinders very nearly departed on this mission. Some had already emplaned. The engines of the transport aircraft were being warmed up. The Company, whose take-off and landing had been necessarily timed to take place ahead of the rest of the Division's, could so easily have been dropped into the heart of the formidable German opposition, before the operation was called off. If that had happened and there had been no follow up, there is little doubt as to the fate of the Company.

Hitler had issued an edict concerning how the Wehrmacht were to deal with parachute troops. They were to be treated as 'franc-tireurs', shot on sight and no prisoners were to be taken. As General Urquhart has commented, 'Wild Oats' would have been 'a very sticky affair'. It was never officially cancelled; merely postponed whilst Intelligence watched for some movement of the enemy from the area. The Company lived with the maps for this operation for some time. It came to know Evrecy and its environs extremely well from a close study of the map and the excellent aerial photographs taken by the RAF but it was never to go there. The writer remembers a church at the top of a hill which would have been one of the rallying points not far from one of the DZs. Again this operation was overtaken by events and naturally fell away as others came from the planners and on to the briefing blackboards.

Operation 'Beneficiary', intended, in conjunction with American land forces, to secure the port of St. Malo in Brittany, involved bringing in the whole of the 1st Air Landing Brigade in gliders by night. There were no suitable landing fields in-shore and it was decided that they would have to be landed on the beach between low and high water marks. A dicey proposition for the pathfinders who stood a very good chance of being dropped either in the sea or on the coast defences. Fortunately, the Royal Navy, responsible for the seaborne landing, found certain objections of their own and at one point wanted the Airborne to undertake not to fire a shot while the sea landings were taking place: clearly an undertaking which could not be made. Since the position was considered too well defended to be cracked from the land alone, 'Beneficiary' joined the ranks of cancelled operations.

'Raising Brittany' might have had interesting possibilities. In this the Company would have led the drop of the Division in the area south of Rennes, forming a base for the Maquis, then, with them under command, operations were to be undertaken against the German flank. Ultimately there was to be a link-up with the Americans moving south from Cherbourg. It never came off. Nor did another operation which in mid-July was intended to open a gap for an armoured break-out of the Caen hinge.

Each operation for which the Company was briefed involved it in travelling south to sealed transit camps, mostly in the Oxford area. From the day of arrival at these tented quarters until take-off or cancellation the Company was held 'prisoner', sometimes for days on end if one cancelled operation was immediately succeeded by another.

When higher authority decided that operations would not be taking place after all, the Company would be given 48 hours' leave either before or after returning to Newark. These 48 hour passes began to be of frequent occurrence as operation followed operation, all aborted. Leave became a source of embarrassment for some.

In Operation 'Hands Up' the target was Vannes and its airfield in Brittany and the aim was to support the westward drive of American armour towards Brest. The Company drew parachutes and were driven to the airfield for this one, but at the last minute came the news: 'The American armour is in Vannes'. Still with their eyes on Brittany the planners produced Operation 'Sword Hilt'. This time a viaduct was to be destroyed and German reserves moving east were to be prevented from plugging the American break-out. But once on the move American armour kept moving and the Airborne again were not needed.

Then came 'Lucky Strike' – a plan for establishing bridge-heads across the Seine, below Rouen, and 'Transfigure', a similar operation, this time near Les Andelys. Either of these might have resulted in the Company being among the first of the Allies to re-enter Paris. There was 'Axehead' and then two operations, 'Linnet' and 'Linnet II' which would have had the Company leading the Division ahead of the advancing 2nd Army in Belgium.

Joe May was one of those who found this succession of aborted operations and the frequent 48 hour leaves embarrassing. More than once he told his pal, Eric (called Bill) Freeman: 'I wish I could get into action. The people up the road where I live keep asking if I've been in action yet.' Unhappily, when Joe did finally get into action he did not return to be able to tell his neighbours 'Yes, I have.'

Operation 'Comet' was the Company's last reprieve. When it was cancelled many of the Company did not even bother to go home on leave, preferring to spend time at the Union Jack Club in London or elsewhere. 'Comet' was the subsequent Operation 'Market' in miniature. The same three dropping areas covering the crossings of the Rivers Maas at Grave, the Waal at Nijmegen and the Neder Rijn at Arnhem. An Airborne Brigade was assigned to each of them and the Company's three pathfinder platoons would have been widely divided in carrying out their tasks. If 'Comet' had taken place 1st Airborne Division would have been the only one engaged, No. 1 Platoon and 1st Parachute Brigade would have gone to Arnhem, 2 and 3 Platoons were assigned to bring in the 4th Parachute Brigade and the 1st Airlanding Brigade respectively in the more southerly areas.

The briefing for 'Comet', which would have taken place in the first week of September, was just two weeks before the

Company actually dropped on Sunday 17 September north of the Lower Rhine between the villages of Heelsum and Wolfhezen about seven miles east of the bridge at Arnhem.

The Company was briefed for Operation 'Market' on Friday 15 September. For No. 1 Platoon it was a repetition of 'Comet'. They would still be bringing in 1st Parachute Brigade on DZ 'X'. The difference was that their comrades in the other two platoons as well as HQ platoon would be not far from them across the Rhine in Holland. Before the Company's ordeal in Holland, however, another operation involving members of the Company took place in mid-August at about the time the pathfinders in England were looking forward, in Operation 'Transfigure', to a triumphal entry into Paris.

7 THE INDEPENDENT PLATOON
1944 – The South of France

It will be remembered that when the Company left Italy for North Africa en route to England in November 1943 it left behind a platoon to form the basis of the pathfinder element to serve the 2nd Independent Parachute Brigade. The platoon became officially known as the 1st Independent Parachute Platoon. It was not only the first but the only Independent Platoon ever!

Under the command of Captain Peter Baker it was a tightly knit unit composed of many of the Larkhill originals, with Sergeants like 'Gremlin' Jones, 'Taffy' Yates, Gus Jones and young Pickering. Lieutenant D'Arifat continued to serve with the platoon for a time and three Lieutenants, one from each of the Battalions, plus a section apiece from their respective Battalions, swelled the strength of Captain Baker's command. 'Dumbo' Willians (4thBn), 'Jock' Boyd (5th Bn), Mike Whiteway (6th Bn) and their men soon became an integral part of the offspring of the parent Company and thus members of the family of pathfinders founded by John Lander and foster-fathered by his successor, Bob Wilson.

For a time the Platoon continued with the 2nd Parachute Brigade in Italy and was then moved to Sicily to train with the US 51st Troop Carrier Wing in all aspects of pathfinding and to gain experience with glider landings. A close and very happy relationship soon developed between the Platoon, the pilots of the Glider Pilot Squadron and the airmen of the carrier wing. Early in 1944 Captain Baker received orders to rejoin the Brigade at Paestum south of Salerno. His unit had benefited considerably from the period spent in Sicily on concentrated flying, parachuting and gliding and in operating the improved pathfinding equipment.

Brigade training now began for what would be the airborne invasion of the South of France which planners were already foreseeing as part of the strategy to follow the main landings in Normandy on D Day. But D Day was still some months away and its date not yet fixed. It is doubtful whether anyone in the 2nd Independent Parachute Brigade, not even its commander Brigadier C. H. V. Pritchard (one time CO of the 6th (royal Welch) Battalion), knew just what their role would be or where they would go into action. Nor could they have had any idea when they would be called upon.

Much of 2nd Brigade had been in action in the Casino sector and elsewhere in Italy operating as infantry. For the best part of two months the three battalions had patrolled the Rapido River watched by the enemy entrenched on Monastery Hill and by the end of May came the launching of a small operation – code name 'Hasty'.

Three officers and 57 other ranks of the 6th Bn were dropped on the evening of 1 June near Torricella. A small section of the Independent Platoon took part in the operation. The purpose was to prevent the Germans carrying out demolitions whilst withdrawing from the Pisa-Rimini line. To deceive the enemy dummy paratroops were also dropped to give the impression of a much larger force.

Brigadier Pritchard's orders to Captain Fitzroy-Smith who commanded the men taking part were 'to occupy the dominating heights by day and descend into the valleys and wreak havoc by night.'

After the drop, the men were concentrated unopposed, but for reasons of concealment were shortly divided into three parties. Each of these parties harassed road communications for a week. As a result of these activities behind German lines, a whole Brigade was moved to deal with what was thought to be a serious threat to German communications whilst a division, which would otherwise have been brought into the line against the 8th Army attack, was ordered to stay where it was.

Other means of communication having failed, Brigadier Pritchard signalled the recall by having leaflets dropped in the area reading 'Proceed Awdry forthwith'. Only men intimately acquainted with the 6th Battalion would know that this referred to one of their officers, John Awdry and understand this message for what it was. On the night of 7 June the personnel of the 'Hasty' operation began to filter back to the Allied lines in twos and threes. About half the number returned.

The D Day landings in Normandy had begun only the day before. 2nd Independent Parachute Brigade and its pathfinders now awaited news of its part in the invasion of France. During June the 2nd Independent Parachute Brigade (and the 1st Independent Parachute Platoon with it) came under the command of US General R. T. Fredericks and became part of the First Airborne Task Force. Apart from the British element the Task Force comprised five battalions of American parachutists and one American glider-borne regiment.

Part of the strategic plan for the invasion of Europe was a subsidiary Allied attack in the South of France timed to coincide with the break-out of the main attack from the Normandy beach-head. From D Day onwards the First Airborne Task Force stood by in and around Rome and the nearby airfields at Ciampino and Galera, awaiting the call to action.

A number of operations were planned, only to be called off. The weeks dragged by and the Independent Platoon must have suffered the same frustrations as the parent Company was doing in England. Release came to the men in Italy with the launching of operation 'Dragoon' (earlier called 'Anvil') on 15 August, a whole month earlier than the operation which would terminate the waiting of their brother pathfinders in England.

'Anvil' had for its prime objective the capture of Marseilles. This was to be followed by a concerted drive up the Rhone valley to join the main Allied sweep into Germany itself. The operation was carried out by the 7th US Army with certain British and French formations under command. The 2nd Independent Parachute Brigade was in fact the only British land formation to take part in the operation.

The seaborne landing took place between Fréjus and Saint-Raphaël, midway between Toulon and Cannes. Little opposition was anticipated in the initial stages but it was believed (and hoped) that considerable German reserves inland would be drawn south to meet the Allied thrust. It was considered necessary to delay any such southward movement until a firm foothold had been gained. The task of imposing this delay was assigned to the First Airborne Task Force. It was a force of some 9732 men, 535 US Army Air Force C 47s and a mixture of 465 British (Hadrians and Horsas) and American (Waco) gliders.

Three dropping and landing zones were selected astride the valley of the Nartuby and Argens rivers. The American Airborne would land in two areas, one near La Motte, the other near Trans-en-Provence. For this purpose they were divided into two groups of brigade strength. The 2nd Independent Parachute Brigade with a glider-borne element including a battery of anti-tank guns were assigned the area of Le Muy in which to land. Americans would do their own pathfinding at La Motte and Trans-en-Provence; the 1st Independent Parachute Platoon would mark the DZ and LZ at Le Muy, where the Brigade was to secure the junction of three roads, destroy what enemy were found in the area and deny the Germans access to the beach-head some 20 miles distant.

The American pathfinders were due to drop first at 03.22 and 03.26 and Captain Baker's Platoon at 03.30, but in fact the Americans were late in dropping and the men of the 1st Independent Parachute Platoon can rightly claim to have been the first of all Allied troops to land in the South of France.

Both Captain Baker and his superior, Brigadier Pritchard, describe the night of the 14/15 August as they left Rome as 'beautiful with the lights of the city twinkling below.' With their Eureka sets and landing lights stowed in kitbags and lashed to strong legs, the pathfinders set out in high spirits for the south of France which few, if any, had seen before. This was one of the strong legs, the pathfinders set out in high spirits for the South of a few hours' flying, in entirely new surroundings, self-reliant in whatever circumstances might be met but equally assured of the reliability of those who dropped with you.

The task to be performed clearly in mind, Captain Baker's men must have carried with them thoughts of emulating the deeds of those who had carried out those earlier D Day landings in France on 6 June. All went well with the British pathfinders, but on crossing the coast of France it was noticed that a thick ground mist obscured the ground below. They jumped exactly on time but blind. They saw nothing until they met the ground among vineyards and olive groves and about a mile from where they needed to be.

Enlisting the aid of locals and in spite of adverse visibility Captain Baker rapidly assembled his men and made for the DZ. Once orientated, the platoon set about its task and the records show that they accurately marked the DZ in good time and had the Eureka working ready to receive the rest of the Brigade at first light. At the same time they busied themselves clearing as many as possible of the anti-glider obstacle poles with which the landing zone was littered. The Brigade was due overhead at 05.00 hours and certainly most of the 106 aircraft were over French territory at that time.

Captain Baker recalls that 'the great majority of the main force landed successfully on target.' Other records show that 73 of the 106 sticks found the DZ, representing about 60% of the 6th Parachute Battalion, 40% of the 4th Parachute Battalion and only one Company of the 5th. Failure to record 100% success was no fault of the pathfinders, however.

Cloud and fog caused some aircraft to lose contact with the lead aircraft equipped with the homing Rebecca. One whole formation carrying the bulk of the 5th Parachute Battalion went astray owing to an electrical fault in the lead aircraft. Unable to pick up the 'Eureka' signal on his Rebecca, the pilot flew on in the hope of finding a break in the cloud. When he finally decided that he must drop his parachutists before long or never get back to base with them, he gave the signal to start dropping, but the lights did not work either. The drop was made in the end on a signal from a flashlight held in the door of the lead aircraft after the lead stick had jumped. It is hardly surprising that the 5th Battalion was scattered over a wide area some 20 miles inland of where they should have been.

It is fortunate that the Germans in the area were not more aggressive or the fate of the 5th Battalion might have been very different to what it was. It took them all that day to reach the rest of the Brigade around Le Muy and what fighting there was was then as good as over.

With the sun rising higher, visibility on the DZ had improved and it was discovered that the landing at Le Muy had been made practically on top of a local German HQ. Indeed, one sergeant of 'B' Company of the 5th Bn had actually landed on its roof. There was, however, little fighting and what there was, was sporadic.

Early contact had been made with the local Maquis, looking like pirates with bits of parachute silk tied around their heads. Their earnestness and resolution impressed those who met them and their presence, as well as the shock of finding paratroops in their midst, must have had something to do with the German reluctance to fight.

Among the early arrivals on the DZ was the Brigade commander who, in spite of being dropped at 1400 feet because of the cloud, landed within 15 yards of the Eureka set. Soon after the fog cleared a heavy concentration of Horsa and Waco gliders arrived and, as always, those on the ground marvelled at the spectacular landings they made in such constricted space.

Unhappily one element of this armada was missing – the heavier-laden gliders bearing the Brigade's anti-tank guns. Whilst the lighter-loaded gliders had been able to hold off over Corsica for the cloud and fog to clear, it had been necessary for the tug aircraft of the heavier gliders to return to base before they ran out of fuel. This they did, casting off gliders over Rome to land once more on the fields they had left hours before. There the gliders were re-marshalled ready for take off, their tow ropes had to be collected and re-attached and the tug aircraft re-fuelled. By a masterly piece of organisation, tugs and gliders took to the air again and arrived in France at 16.30 hours after a total of six hours' towing that day.

The absence of the guns during those crucial first 12 hours could have had serious repercussions if there had been any German tanks in the area. This serves to illustrate the hazards which parachute troops always face. Seaborne forces made contact with the airborne within 24 hours. Fighting had been only sporadic and casualties light. The pathfinder platoon sustained one fatality – Terry Morley, one of the young 'originals', whose parachute failed to function. Within a short time the 1st Independent Parachute Platoon was back in Italy, having embarked by sea at Toulon.

If anyone goes to the museum at Toulon today they will find on exhibition a parachutist's smock and jumping boots. They belonged to Peter Baker, almost certainly the first of the Allied officers to land in the South of France in operation 'Dragoon'.

The Americans had had their share of problems on the day. Twenty-nine 'planeloads of infantry and artillery of the 509th Parachute Infantry Regiment were dropped by mistake about three miles from St. Tropez near German coastal defences. The paratroops found themselves not only dealing with Germans but in the middle of the sea-and-air bombardment intended to soften up the defence before the seaborne assault. Having weathered the storm (incidentally, without casualties, so it could not have been too bad) they got five guns into action and succeeded in capturing intact two coastal batteries, one flak battery and about 240 Germans! They then entered St. Tropez well ahead of the seaborne troops. This is thought to be the only example in World War II of a direct parachute assault to overwhelm beach defences – by mistake.

It has been suggested (in retrospect) that the South of France landings were a mistake in that they failed to draw a sufficient German reaction and that the airborne effort brought too small a return. It is said that this was the penalty for acting upon inaccurate information as to enemy intentions, which led to over-cautious planning, and that the reluctance of the Allies to take risks stemmed from the fierce and effective German reactions to the Allied landings at Anzio and Salerno.

Howsoever all this may be, the fact remains that for the airborne soldier, and more especially the pathfinder, any operation into enemy territory is a hazardous business, a leap into the unknown, blessed with good fortune maybe, as in this case, or dogged by ill-fortune, as at Arnhem. Called upon to jump, the pathfinder never knew just what fate awaited him below. He jumped just the same.

An interesting background account to 'Anvil' later named 'Dragoon' is to be found in Chapter 4 of Volume II of Sir Winston Churchill's account of the Second World War.

8 ARNHEM
17 September to 26 September 1944 Operation 'Market'

The story of the Arnhem battle has been told so many times that it hardly seems necessary to repeat that the object of operation 'Market Garden' was to gain access to Germany beyond the Rhine so that an offensive inside Germany itself could be launched before winter set in.

It is well known that this was meant to be achieved by Montgomery's 2nd Army in the shape of 30 Corps breaking out of its position behind the Meuse-Escaut Canal on the Belgian-Dutch border south of Eindhoven. It involved a 64-mile dash straight up the single stretch of road via Eindhoven, Grave and Nijmegen to the final river crossing at Arnhem. To facilitate the progress of 30 Corps an 'airborne carpet', as Montgomery termed it, was to be laid securing the bridges and river crossings at the three last-named places.

The American 82nd and 101st Airborne Divisions were to take care of all crossings up to and including Nijmegen. The British 1st Airborne Division and the Polish Airborne Brigade had the task of securing the Arnhem bridge which was vital to the success of the operation as a whole. It was anticipated that the spearhead of 30 Corps, the Guards Armoured Brigade, would make contact with the 1st Airborne Division in Arnhem within 48 hours or at latest on D plus 4.

That they failed to do so is a melancholy fact of British military history. That the Arnhem Bridge was valiantly held for four crucial days by Colonel Johnny Frost and his small number of parachutists is also a fact.

This account is not intended to be a critical analysis of the operation. That has been done many times by authors sufficiently far removed from the action, both in time and in space, to be able to regard the concept and execution of 'Market Garden' dispassionately. Nor will this account seek to tell the story of what befell the many splendid units of the 1st Airborne Division except so far as it touches upon and directly relates to the part played by the 21st Independent Parachute Company.

This then is Operation 'Market' – the airborne aspect of 'Market Garden' – as carried out by the pathfinders north of the Neder Rijn on 17 September 1944. It was an operation which began with high hopes and complete confidence not only in the Division's own fighting ability but in the dash of the Guards Armoured and the qualities of General Brian Horrocks' 30 Corps. Failure did not even remotely cross the minds of the Company's 186 officers and men.

The Company had been in a water-logged sealed transit camp for days prior to that beautiful Sunday morning and were more than ready to go. Another cancellation at this stage might have led to serious deterioration of morale. Already there had been signs of this manifested in brawls with Americans in pubs and attacks on military police who tried to intervene. The latter occasions usually resulted in Americans and airborne uniting against the common enemy. In the Company there had been a breach of security when one man had disclosed his packet of 'escape' money in Oxford and tried to dispose of it. Only the launching of the operation saved him from the inevitable court-martial.

As soon as it looked certain that the operation was on, however, morale attained its old heights. Sergeant Jim Travis, who had broken a small bone in his wrist and had his arm in a plaster cast, insisted on jumping and the CO, knowing his value, agreed to his going with No. 1 Platoon.

In the case of Private Eric Freeman he was not so persuaded. Freeman reported sick, the day before the Company was due to fly, with a septic heel resulting from a previous injury. When Bob Wilson learned of this, he sent for Freeman and told him 'I'll be leaving you here. I don't want to start off with a liability. I'm sorry but you will understand that every man must be able to take care of himself once we are on the ground.' Freeman accepted this ruling with good grace though disappointed. When he learned that the injured sergeant was to be allowed to jump he felt otherwise. There is, however, an obvious difference between a sergeant with an injured arm and a private whose ability to march is suspect. In fact, Jim Travis went right through the action with his arm in plaster and, trying though it must have been, performed his duties with commendable competence.

At 10.00 hours on that fine Sunday morning the Company took off from Fairford airfield in 12 Stirling bombers converted for the dropping of parachutists. The exit aperture was a large coffin-shaped hole in the floor and to the rear of the fuselage. The Company had never jumped from Stirlings before and stick commanders were required to organise their jump-order to suit the aircraft to their needs. At least four men in each Stirling jumped with full, heavily-laden kitbags strapped to their legs. There was room in the wide body of the Stirling to group the kitbag men near and around the aperture. They would, of necessity, be the first to jump.

Most stick commanders chose to jump in the middle order of the 'stick' and to have a senior NCO at the back of the stick to jump last. The purpose of this was to facilitate a fast jump and a speedy re-organisation on the ground, the men moving up the line to the kitbag men to assist with their loads. Before take-off stick commanders discussed with RAF navigators the precise point on the DZ over which the drop should commence. This was done by reference to the first-class large-scale maps of the area carried by all the pathfinder leaders and by consulting aerial photographs.

On that first day one DZ and two LZs were to be marked. DZ 'X' for the reception of 1st Parachute Brigade was the task of No. 1 Platoon. No. 1 Section was detailed to do the actual marking with panels spelling out the 'X' and a 'T' for wind direction as well as the working of the Eureka beacon and smoke canisters. But as in all platoons, the equipment was triplicated so that if anything went awry with No. 1 Section any of the others could perform the task. Section commanders were in touch with their platoon commanders by short range 'walkie-talkie' sets.

No. 2 Platoon had the task of marking LZ 'Z' for the glider landing of support elements of 1st Parachute Brigade such as 1 Anti-Tank Battery RA, 1 Parachute Squadron RE and 16 Field

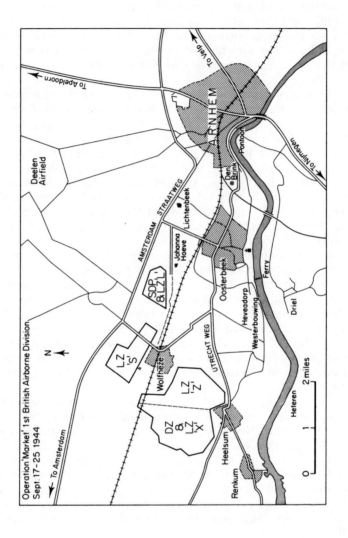

Operation 'Market' 1st British Airborne Division
Sept. 17-25 1944

To Amsterdam →

N →

To Apeldoorn →

Deelen Airfield

AMSTERDAM STRAATWEG

LZ 'S'

SDP & LZ 'L'

Johanna Hoeve

Lichtenbeek

Wolfheze

DZ & LZ 'X'

LZ 'Z'

Renkum

Heelsum

UTRECHT WEG

Oosterbeek

Heveadorp

Westerbouwing

Ferry

Heteren

Driel

Den Brink

Pontoon

ARNHEM

To Velp →

To Nijmegen →

0   1   2 miles

Ambulance RAMC. LZ 'Z' lay parallel with but east of DZ 'X' and separated from it by a belt of trees. Thick forest areas also lined the western edge of DZ 'X' and it was necessary to site Eureka well clear of the trees so that the beam was not interfered with and, since there was a mild breeze from the east, the drop point had to be marked well to the east to prevent parachutes drifting into the woods.

There was plenty of width to the DZ and both DZ and LZ had a clear length of over a mile stretching from Heelsum to the railway line at their northern extremity. These were ideal landing areas except for their distance from the main objective.

The second LZ (LZ 'S') lay to the north of the railway line which ran east to west between Arnhem and Utrecht. Here No. 3 Platoon and Company HQ would land and mark it to receive the greater part of 1st Airlanding Brigade in their gliders. There would be further pathfinder tasks for the Company on the second and third days, but for the moment attention was rivetted on the success of the first day.

The Company's War Diary records:

'. . . the journey (from Fairford to the DZs) was almost uneventful, with the exception of a little light flak fired at one aircraft of No. 1 Platoon. 13.00 hours. Platoons were most accurately dropped in correct places and what little opposition there was was quickly overcome. Navigational aids were immediately set out and twenty minutes later the first gliders appeared. The landings were effected without opposition and all the gliders reported that they had no difficulty in seeing the markings of their correct areas. 13.45 hours. The 1st Parachute Brigade were dropped on DZ 'X'. The drop was accurate and Battalions were well together. So far the enemy has made no serious attempt to interfere with the landings. During the course of the afternoon some enemy opposition was encountered but the DZ and LZs were kept clear. The night was quiet. All the Company was concentrated round HQ at farm Reijers Camp.'

The landings had, indeed, gone well. Better in fact than any previous exercise on this scale. The Company had carried out its pathfinder role in a manner which would have gratified its founder, the late John Lander.

There was one incident on DZ 'X' which at first gave the impression that No. 1 Platoon was under attack by mortars: a series of explosions which sent up black smoke not far from where the 'Eureka' was sited. It turned out to be a canister of mortar bombs which had had a bad landing, caught fire and was now the cause of bombs detonating as the heat reached them or by sympathetic detonation of one bomb after another. Fortunately the canister lay in a hollow and no harm was done. Nevertheless it was a spot to be avoided.

On LZ 'Z' No. 2 Platoon and the Company sustained its first fatality. Indeed, Corporal James Arthur Jones was almost certainly the first man in the Division to die in the Arnhem operation. Accidentally shot through the head, he died instantly, soon after landing.

Not recorded in the Company War Diary was General Urquhart's recollections of landing by glider on LZ 'S'. He says:
'So confident was the Independent Company about the outcome that they had taken quantities of metal and boot polish for the liberation celebrations and the victorious entry into Germany. Wilson had packed his best battledress and highly polished brown shoes into his parachutist's leg-bag which also contained one bottle each of whisky, gin and sherry for the entertainment of Dutch resistance leaders. The leg-bag weighed 75 pounds and the liquor was intact when 'Boy' landed.'

In his book *Arnhem* he also notes that the pathfinders jumped 'falling through sparse small-arms fire. One of the men who was hit was unhurt, although a bullet passed through his chest haversack which held mortar bombs.' He also mentions one man being hit in the air and dying. This almost certainly refers to Corporal Jones, but is mistaken. His death came after landing in the circumstances mentioned above.

Of the opposition referred to in the War Diary, General Urquhart says, 'Wilson struggled clear of his harness to find himself face to face with a surrendering German, who led him to a foxhole occupied by other members of the Wehrmacht who saw little point in fighting. They had been having lunch when the attack began.' They were told to hang on while he organised his task force.

A release of carrier pigeons to carry the news of unopposed landing got no further than the nearest roof of a farm building until a few well aimed pebbles saw the birds on their way to England. The General also writes that a quarter of an hour before the first gliders were due the Company were in position, 'with one casualty, 16 prisoners and its first booty – a German staff car.' When the gliders began to land Bob Wilson, recognising one pilot as an old friend, offered him a drink of water. At the farmhouse, the CO opened his whisky bottle unseen by the glider pilot who, on tasting this hospitality, said, 'My God, this Dutch water's good!'

So passed the first few hours of the operation. That night the platoons were well dug in in soft, rich, soot-black soil, in all-round protection of Company HQ at Reijers Camp. The first brew of tea and a hot meal of boullion (from concentrated cakes of the stuff) with hard biscuits was prepared from the individual 48-hour ration packs of concentrated food each man carried. The heat required was provided by the tiny folding stoves burning solid methylated fuel which was both flameless and smokeless. In the direction of Arnhem sounds of battle, MG and mortar fire could be heard, but gradually died away as the dark moonless night descended.

With the dawn of Monday 18 September came fresh tasks for the pathfinders and their second day in action. The Company War Diary notes:

'Platoons moved out during the morning to mark DZ and LZs for the second lift. No. 1 Platoon to LZ 'L', No. 2 Platoon to LZ 'X' and No. 3 Platoon to DZ 'Y'. HQ remained on 'S' to supply aids. Enemy opposition was encountered in all landing areas and platoons had stiff fighting to drive the enemy back and to hold them whilst the second lift landed, also having to put out ground aids under fire.'

On LZ 'L' the best part of a mile from Reijers Camp, No. 1 Platoon had a long wait for the supply drop due at 10.00 hours. Though the weather overhead seemed clear enough it was otherwise over the airfields in England, but the Company had no way of knowing this. Around midday a number of enemy fighters flew overhead, banked in the east and came back strafing the platoon. They caused no casualties though coming very close to hitting the Eureka set which, to function, had to be sited out in the open clear of the trees which surrounded the LZ.

No. 1 Section, placed some distance east of platoon HQ to cover a concealed approach, had visitors during the day. First, a number of civilians moving west to escape the battle area. Next, three men of 1st Battalion, one an officer who the night before had dived into what he thought was a foxhole but which was in fact a sewage pit. He was decent enough to sit down-wind when he stopped to give Sergeant Kent news of what was going on with 1st Parachute Battalion's attempt to break into Arnhem. It did not sound very promising and he was passed on to David Eastwood at platoon HQ. Sounds were even less promising when a tracked vehicle was heard approaching from the east with its heavy slow engine beat and screeching tracks: all very menacing, but it remained concealed by the thick bush and trees in the area.

It was not until 15.30 hours that the roar of multiple aero-engines signalled the approach of the long-awaited supply drop and the storm of flak and machine gun fire put up by the enemy. This came as something of a surprise after the lack of such a reception the day before. The Germans had obviously reacted very quickly to yesterday's landings. Soon the supply panniers and canisters were showering down, accurately guided By Eureka and the pathfinders' marker strips, which had, of course, given the position away to the Luftwaffe.

Similar experiences befell the other platoons. Though the flak was probably heaviest over LZ 'L' they both had a torrid time. No. 3 Platoon on DZ 'Y' were a good four miles to the west, bringing in the 4th Parachute Brigade, and the drop was made under heavy ground fire, and a stiff breeze had sprung up. Some men landed in trees, but quickly extricated themselves. On landing, 11th Parachute Battalion alone took some 80 prisoners, which is an indication of the German presence about the DZ. On the whole, however, the pathfinders had once again done all that could be reasonably required of them.

No. 2 Platoon, on the other LZ just below Reijers Camp, also experienced the attention of ME 109's, but brought in the remainder of 1st Air Landing Brigade and further Divisional Troops.

The War Diary continues:

'The Company rendezvoused at 18.00 hours at the farm and moved at 19.00 hours to take up new positions in the area of Halt Oosterbeek Hoig. The move was carried out without casualties or opposition in the dark and the new position was established by 23.00 hours. A horse and dray was commandeered to move heavy equipment. The night was uneventful.'

It had been a long hard day with little time for rest. The march from Reijers Camp was a slow, stop-start business, far more tiring than any straight-forward route march and over a comparatively short distance on the map. This will be seen from the time indicated by the War Diary. During the day there had been the march to and from the LZs and DZ as well as the nervous energy expended on the landing areas, digging in, being strafed and generally helping wherever needed. The Airborne

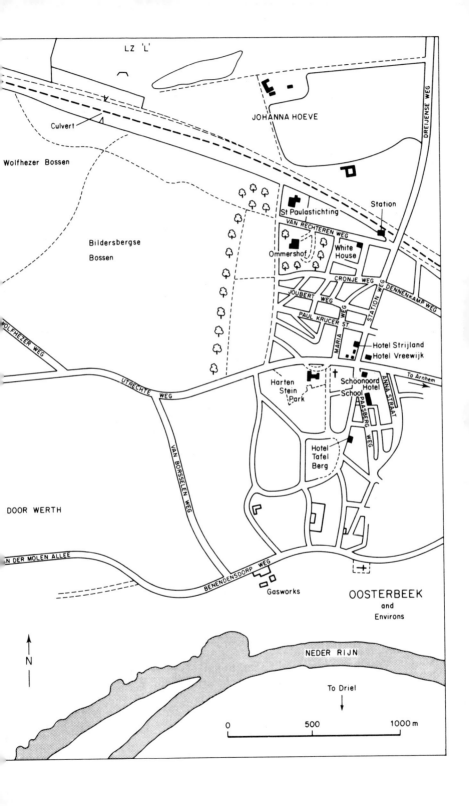

RASC had very smartly cleared the LZ of supplies rushing hither and thither in their jeeps with trailers.

That night the Company lay in the grounds of a large house, 'St Paulastichting', with Company HQ in the house itself. Though the night was described as uneventful the Company lay for a time under very heavy machine gun fire from the other side of the railway line: a fine display of tracer bullets winging away, mostly far too high, but at times close enough to crack and whine and to make it advisable to keep one's head down.

It was a cold, uncomfortable night spent in the open under hedges. A brew of tea was possible at Reijers Camp before the march began, but that was all there was time for, for most, until next morning.

'No. 1 Platoon moved out again to DZ 'L' to supply navigational aids for the third lift, i.e., the Polish Glider element. They beat off a heavy enemy attack when the gliders were landing. No. 2 Platoon supplied aids for the supply drop.' So begins the Company's War Diary for Tuesday 19 September.

This, the third day of the action, was one of feverish activity for the Company, and for No. 1 Platoon in particular, who had to move in sections from cover to cover through the wooded rides bordering the railway line through what was then a no man's land but which during the day became held by the enemy.

The distance from Company HQ to where the platoon set up its landing aids was about a mile and a half and rather more than a mile to the point where a culvert under the embanked railway gave access to the strip of woodland bordering the LZ just north of the line. As on the day before the time of arrival of the third lift was 10.00 hours. Although the LZ itself was familiar, from yesterday's experience, the approach to it was new and had to be carefully reconnoitred. No. 1 Section, invariably chosen as point section, led the way.

The same dispositions were made as for the previous day, save that the Eureka team found an accommodating dung heap under cover of which to operate! Half an hour before the estimated time of arrival of the gliders, Tommy McMahon and his mate were out and ready to operate. The rest of the platoon were in defensive positions and, in view of yesterday's strafing, began digging in.

Unknown to the platoon, the Germans were now in possession of the full operational plan for the Arnhem operation thanks to some idiot who, in spite of the words 'Not to be taken in the air' plastered all over them, landed with them in his glider, which was captured on landing, and was sufficiently close to General Student's HQ in a cottage at Vught for them to be in his hands within two hours of the original landings. The Germans probably knew all about LZ 'L' and the Polish glider-borne troops due to land there. They made their dispositions accordingly, as No. 1 Platoon and the unfortunate Poles and their glider pilots would later discover.

The morning dragged on past 10.00 hours and was enlivened by further visits from Messerschmitts who beat up the platoon's positions in three or four waves. Apart from scaring the living daylights out of everyone lying under the stream of bullets from the fast moving 'planes only metres off the ground, they did no harm. The platoon remained where it was and dug in just that little bit deeper. These passes by the enemy fighters were of short, sharp duration and each time they passed heads would slowly appear, look around, and grin sheepishly at one another.

There is nothing really funny about being shot at in this way. In fact, one feels rather foolish and helpless to be lying down under it. After the second or third wave a few bold souls lay on their backs in their slit trenches and fired their weapons straight up in the air in the forlorn hope that the odd bullet might prove unlucky for some German pilot. As far as is known, neither side damaged the other. This aerial attention had the merit of giving the platoon something to do (mostly digging) while awaiting the arrival of the Poles.

Down at his forward outpost Sergeant Kent of No. 1 Section had mustered together some stragglers from the 1st Air Landing Brigade (who according to the Divisional plan were supposed to be in defence of the LZ) under a sergeant and asked David Eastwood's permission to hand over his position to them and rejoin the platoon. This was granted and the section arrived there on the west side of the LZ near the southern corner of it just in time for the last strafing by the ME's before the third lift arrived. No slit trenches having been dug for the section, there was overcrowding of other peoples' 'fox-holes' as the section dived for cover. The alternative, which some were left with, was to get behind impossibly thin and totally inadequate young trees.

A sense of humour was always a strong feature within the Company and soon after the danger had passed, leaving the place stinking of cordite, there was some chaffing and laughter provoked by the ludicrous situations in which members of the section had found themselves. The section promptly took up a sector covering a 'ride' in the woods behind platoon HQ in a small clearing just off the LZ and dug in.

The third lift arrived late, as on the previous day, about mid-afternoon. Just before the Polish gliders arrived a message was received from Divisional HQ, instructing the pathfinders to get out on the LZ as soon as the gliders landed and redirect the Poles to Oosterbeek. When they had left England their orders were, it seems, to make straight for Arnhem.

The arrival of the big, black-winged Horsas with their blue and white striped markings was the signal for the Germans to open up with everything they had. With flak, far thicker than the day before, overhead and mortar and machine gun fire on the ground, the landing gliders met a hail of fire. A similar reception greeted the supply drop being brought in by No. 2 Platoon some distance away.

Although the original SDP was no longer available because the enemy held it, every effort was made to redirect the dropping aircraft on to a site where the supplies would reach the RASC crews waiting to bring them in. The message to the RAF changing the SDP had not got through, however. Now in the area of the SDP the 156th Battalion and the 10th Battalion were preparing to attack Lichtenbeek. They made little progress and No. 2 Platoon had to watch helplessly as aircraft after aircraft flying at a few hundred feet through the storm of flak dropped their loads into enemy-held territory.

No. 2 Platoon, in common with others in the Divisional perimeter, witnessed heroic feats of flying as the slow-moving, laden aircraft flew steadfastly on to carry out the planned drop in face of deadly anti-aircraft fire, the heaviest yet seen. Nearly all in vain. Precious supplies of ammunition, food and medical equipment fell into enemy hands. The RASC salvaged what they could, aided by No. 2 Platoon, at considerable personal risk.

163 aircraft flew that mission. 13 were shot down and 97 others were more or less seriously hit. None turned back. All delivered their loads. No. 2 Platoon with less distance to cover than No. 1 Platoon had done its best and returned to the Company position before light failed.

The War Diary continues:

'During the afternoon the enemy started a movement on the Company position and I (Major Wilson) decided to take up a new position on some high ground overlooking the previous one, which gave us a field of fire approximately one hundred and fifty yards and forced the enemy to attack uphill across a road with wire fencing. The Company dug in to the grounds of a house called "Ommershof". We were reinforced by two officers and thirty men of the 4th Parachute Field Squadron, RE, and some sixty glider pilots under Major Jackson.'

On LZ 'L' the Germans unleashed a vicious attack with MG and mortar fire upon hapless Poles and glider pilots who had left England expecting to push straight into Arnhem and who now were the survivors of the flak storm ahead. Few of the gliders landed unscathed. Some broke up in the air, scattering already wounded men on to the LZ. Some, their pilots killed or wounded, crashed into each other or crashed on landing. Others, riddled with flak, disintegrated with the impact of landing.

Through all this and the withering MG and mortar fire the men of No. 1 Platoon hared around among the surviving Poles and pilots directing them south of the strip of woodland bordering the railway line which at that point was embanked. Here, more confusion reigned. Troops were streaming along the railway below the embankment going westward towards Wolfhezen – away from Arnhem! It looked like a retreat.

Soon after the landings, and before the Poles could orientate themselves, the Germans began probing down through the woods and rides from the north towards No. 1 Platoon's position. Here considerable execution was done by the three Bren guns, rifle and Sten gun fire of the platoon and the glider pilots. David Eastwood must have known of the westward movement of the troops in rear of the platoon along the railway line. He sent Sergeant Kent off there to try to raise a counter-attack. With sniper Paddy Gamble at his heels he tore through the belt of woodland, keeping low, with Germans clearly visible behind him coming on to No. 1 Platoon's position. He found an officer in the rather defeated-looking shambles, but the latter was not interested in pulling any chestnuts out of anyone else's fire. 'My orders are to get back to Wolfhezen and re-group and that's where we're going,' he said, and marched on. It seemed that No. 1 Platoon was the only organised resistance north of the railway and it probably was.

The platoon's fire power seemed to have dampened the enemy's enthusiasm, but not for long. In the lull in the firing German voices could be heard in the woods rallying their troops for another excursion down through the woods. On learning that no counter-attack would be forthcoming, David Eastwood decided it was time to leave.

It was clear that the platoon could not return to the Company position by the route it had taken that morning. The platoon was cut off in that direction. With No. 1 Section again point section, the platoon headed south, climbed the railway embankment now under MG fire and were held up. Here an enthusiastic but misguided Polish major tried to press-gang some of the platoon into manhandling an abandoned anti-tank gun into position on the railway line itself. He only desisted when it was pointed out that it had no breech-block and no ammunition, anyway!

The platoon crossed the railway and plunged down the embankment on the other side, forcing a way into a fairly heavy woodland beyond. Heading south for the main Utrecht-Arnhem road it hoped to make contact with friendly troops outside the Divisional perimeter. No such luck. All that was found were the bodies of dead Germans scattered here and there.

The silence which now prevailed seemed more menacing than the noise of battle. As the platoon emerged from the trees on to the deserted road junction the silence was broken by the ghostly whoosh and wail of shells sailing overhead to explode in the Wolfhezen area.

During the day, General Urquhart had ordered the withdrawal of Brigadier Hackett's 4th Parachute Brigade to Wolfhezen to re-group and to take a southerly approach towards Arnhem. This was quite unknown to No. 1 Platoon at the time. They were now in an eerie no-man's land between the Divisional perimeter and the re-grouping at Wolfhezen.

Also unknown was the fact that the 4th Parachute Brigade, which had had a very hard fight that day, arrived at Wolfhezen comprised of only 250 officers and men of 10th Parachute Battalion and 270 of the 156th Battalion. 11th Battalion seems to have disintegrated in the course of this day's heavy fighting.

For a brief moment David Eastwood seemed uncertain whether to try to get back into the Oosterbeek perimeter or head for Wolfhezen to join 4th Parachute Brigade. In those moments there were some in the platoon who had visions of having to head for the river and swim for it that night.

David Eastwood's mind was made up when an officer in a jeep came speeding round a bend in the road from Oosterbeek making for Wolfhezen. He came to a screeching halt when signalled and after a brief chat, Lieutenant Eastwood told the point section to head for Oosterbeek. Within the Divisional lines in and around Oosterbeek, General Urquhart remembers 'Boy' Wilson waiting to report. He says in his book:

'Characteristically, he oozed optimism; this grandfather of paratroopers positively glowed in battle. "They've been trying to tell us all the time you were a prisoner, sir" he said cheerfully. "We told 'em we didn't believe it." "You haven't been talking to these people, have you?" I said. "That's just it" he said. "We have." The Germans had brought up a loud-speaker through which they had blared the somewhat garbled information that I was a prisoner and that what was left of the Division was now surrounded. "It is better you should give yourselves up Tommy." Wilson's men answered with a Bren gun burst. They had enjoyed little respite since the initial landings, though the way Wilson described it they were finding life anything but uncongenial. "They were terrified of the red berets" Wilson exulted. "They don't like us one bit".'

Meantime, No. 1 Platoon were still out on the road, cautiously moving back towards Oosterbeek. Just before dusk the platoon passed through the lines of Border Regiment and soon after found the Company's position at Ommershof. It was allotted a sector facing west, with glider pilots on its left and No. 2 Platoon at right angles to it on the right (northern) flank. The platoon dug in, in two-man weapon slits beneath the cover of trees and shrubs and a high wire fence which separated it from a track wide enough to take a jeep. Beyond the track lay the open stretch of grassland which sloped away to the north and was to become the platoon's killing ground. On the far side of this, 150 yards away, was woodland.

It had been a ghastly day and the men in the weapon pits (which were improved as the night wore on) took turns to watch and to rest. Most had not eaten very much all day and water was scarce. The Company War Diary for the day concludes:– 'The enemy did not make any serious attempt to attack during hhe night but patrols were active.' No. 1 Platoon were spared these patrols. As the War Diary says: 'No. 1 Platoon, who had been cut off, rejoined soon after darkness and occupied the line as shown on the sketch map.'

Unfortunately, no sketch map accompanied the author's copy of the War Diary, but from his own recollection and other sources he has been able to produce the one appearing on page 101.

The day just passed had seen the last of the Company's pathfinding activities. Although, according to the original Divisional orders, the Company was intended to mark DZ 'K' on the other side of the river south-west of the Arnhem bridge for the Polish Parachute Brigade, it was now clear that no part of the Company could get across to do it. In addition, though few of the Company knew it, the DZ for the Poles had been changed to just east of Driel opposite the open river end of the Division's horseshoe perimeter around Oosterbeek.

Now on Wednesday 20 September the full Company took up its new role, started yesterday, as part of the perimeter defence. It was a perimeter which was to shrink as the days wore on. As the action entered the fourth day it was a case of digging in deeper and being ready to repulse anything the enemy sent against the position. The options were his not ours. About 09.00 hours a mortar 'stonk' began on the Company's positions which, with more or less intensity, continued at intervals through the day.

At 10.00 hours, the Company's War Diary records: 'The enemy tried to cross the road to the right of our position.' This was on No. 2 Platoon's front and part of 3 Platoon was also engaged in a fire-fight which inflicted heavy casualties on the Germans and some on the defenders. Amongst the latter was Sergeant Stan Brown, who was shot through both arms, the bullets narrowly missing his chest.

'They also moved up on the left flank through the woods evacuated by the Borderers on the previous night.' Here No. 1 Platoon was engaged and had some good shooting. As one sergeant observed: 'They need to give some attention to their fieldcraft', since they could be both seen and heard moving about on the fringe of the wood opposite No. 1 Platoon and the glider pilots.

The mortaring intensified from time to time and the fragmentation caused by tree-bursts caused the Company casualties to mount as the day progressed. It was a remarkably confused day. There have been varying accounts of the same incidents. Some aver that certain things happened on that day; others, obviously speaking of the same incident, think that it occurred on the following day. This is hardly surprising. Everyone was dog tired. No one had had his clothes or boots off since the landing on Sunday. The view was limited to what could be seen at ground level peering out of slit trenches. Brains were constantly assaulted by explosions. There was little of the 48-hour ration pack left to eat. Its contents had been eked out over three days already. Sleep, such as was possible, had been intermittent and taken in the cramped confines of holes in the ground. It was little wonder then that one man's recollection of any particular incident should differ both in content and sequence to another's.

Sifting the accounts, this is an attempt to set down what actually happened that day so far as concerns the 21st Independent Parachute Company now fighting as infantry in the line. The bare bones of the day are recorded tersely in the War Diary. After noting that the morning attacks were 'repulsed with heavy losses' it says: 'Later in the day, he (the enemy) attacked approximately one company strong supported by mortars and an S.P. gun which was knocked out by us with a PIAT.' What happened was this. At some stage in the afternoon, during a lull in the mortar fire, the Germans shouted across to the Company something about 'surrender'. It was not clear just who was meant to surrender to whom. Corporal Max Rodley, one of No. 1 Platoon's German-speaking Jewish personnel, called back in German to induce them to come into the open.

General Urquhart, in his book, mentions this incident in the following terms:
'At some stage, the Germans called on the Independent Company to surrender and Wilson ordered one of his German-speaking troops to reply broadly on the lines that the Company was too scared to venture out and that the Germans should send a party to fetch them. Wilson ordered his men to stand by. None-the-less, he was surprised when about 50 Germans emerged from the wood across the open field. Twelve Brens opened up simultaneously and not a German escaped.' It was certainly not as clear-cut as that.

Bill Mollett of No. 1 Platoon merely says: 'Got another cert. when a bunch of Jerries came right out into the open in front of us. Also several possibles. Max tried to get them to surrender and they tried to get us to do the same. Eastwood's famous words: "Tell them we'll give them a minute." ' No. 1 Section's sergeant, Ron Kent, recalls telling his section to hold fire as the Germans began to emerge. His intention was to let them get close before ordering rapid fire. He wanted none to escape. David Eastwood, as Platoon commander, was also calling for the withholding of fire. Possibly he thought the Germans were surrendering to the Company, though this is doubtful.

They were armed, carried no indication of surrender and did not raise their hands. Maybe he had the same notion as the sergeant or, on the contrary, did not like the deception which would put the enemy at our mercy. The incident was never discussed afterwards, but when Bren guns opened up from the glider pilots on 1 Platoon's left the platoon was quick to take up and join in the carnage. The Germans went to ground; either hit or for cover. Some could be seen crawling back for the cover of the woods.

In the view of No. 1 Section's sergeant, fire was opened prematurely and he did not hear David Eastwood's 'Tell them we'll give them a minute' and has no idea at what juncture this was said. He does remember seeing his platoon officer grim and whitefaced, calling for 'Cease fire' shortly after the firing began. The whole thing was somehow unsatisfactory.

Although the Company was never again subjected to aerial attack, as on previous days, the absence of any Allied air local support was missed and remarked upon. It would have helped the defenders tremendously if they could have seen a few rocket-firing Typhoons and Tempests directed on to targets of their choice. They certainly would not have felt so alone and abandoned. As General Urquhart remarks: '. . . there was no direct signal link between either RAF HQ controlling the operation or Brereton's Allied Airborne HQ and 2nd Tactical Air Force.' The 1st Airborne Division suffered greatly throughout the operation by reason of this neglect, for which more than one senior officer in the chain of command must stand accused.

Soon after 'the killing ground affair', the Germans brought up an SP gun which began shelling the Company at short range over open sights. It was no more than 200 yards away. After No. 2 Platoon had had a go at it with MG and mortar fire, Private Landon of No. 2 Platoon left his position to stalk the gun with his PIAT and succeeded in putting it out of action. To make sure, he went forward still further and was cut down by German machine gun fire.

This was but one of the many gallant acts of the Company's Jewish contingent. Landon, whose true name was Walter Schwartz, had lived on the famous Unter den Linden in Berlin before the war. He died of his wounds at Company HQ.

There came a further attempt on the part of the enemy to persuade the Company to surrender. It came in a strange, unreal fashion. Mortaring stopped, the shooting died. Into the unaccustomed silence came the jingling sound of music. It reminded some of childhood days when musical icecream cars used to come through the streets in summer. The music gave place to a metallic voice which came loud and clear through a loudspeaker. 'Men of the 1st Airborne Division', it said, 'the game is up.

Surrender now. Come out waving a white handkerchief. You have two minutes to decide whether you live or die. Surrender. Or tonight will be your last night on earth. You will never see your wives and sweethearts again. Your comrades are being slaughtered. Your tanks will never reach you.'

It was eerie listening to that disembodied voice. A silence greeted this message – but only for a few seconds. Rude, farting sounds were heard from the beleaguered Company which quickly grew into a storm of abusive language. Some, in true Army style, invited the speaker to go and perform an impossible sexual act. Amid the jeers a voice was heard 'Where the f . . . ing hell does he think we're going to find a white handkerchief.'

It could be expected that all hell would now be let loose but apart from renewed mortar fire, to which the Company had become accustomed, nothing happened. All the Company War Diary says is: 'During the evening the enemy called upon us to surrender. The night was comparatively quiet.'

Elsewhere in the Divisional area casualties were building up. At dusk a plan was made to make a last effort to reach Johnny Frost at the bridge. It failed as had all previous attempts. The Germans had too strong a wedge between the men at the bridge and the encircled Division's remnants. It was just not humanly possible to get through. Too many had died trying.

The Company's near neighbours, the KOSB's were in houses along the Graaf van Rechteren Weg. Its HQ occupied what was called 'the White House'. They had not been bothered so much as the Company that day. Their turn was soon to come.

Little or no news reached the Company as to how far the 2nd Army had got, but it was still believed that the bridge was held and that they would reach the Division eventually. That night the gallant resistance at the bridge came to an agonised end, but the Company was not to know this.

The battle entered the fifth day with the Company still holding its position at Ommershof. The Company War Diary reads: '07.00 hours. The enemy attacked early and a fairly large force was seen to be moving up the wood on our left flank. Mortaring was heavy.' Though there was movement in the woods across No. 1 Platoon's front, there was no attack as such mounted against it from that direction. No attempt was made, as on the previous day, to cross the open stretch of field separating the platoon from the enemy.

Snipers were very active and limited the platoon's movement which, in any case, was minimal – a member of each section collecting waterbottles to refill them at a tap in the house. Paddy Redmond performed this task for No. 1 Section of 1 Platoon. Company HQ was accommodated in the house. Most of the Company had lived out in the open for four days and nights.

The morning was not marked by any special incident. The same could not be said of the afternooon. It was full of them. At one stage, the enemy brought up what No. 1 Platoon observers describe as 'some sort of field gun' in the far corner of the 'killing ground' – the north-west corner. The Company War Diary talks of 'an SP gun brought up on our left flank caused some casualties until knocked out by No. 1 Platoon and the Sappers.' It was certainly put out of action by No. 1 Platoon – just about everyone had a go at it – the three Bren gunners, Tommy Morgan, Jock Avalon and Darkie Roberts in particular had a hand in silencing this new menace. Just as certainly, it was not a self-propelled gun. A truck was later brought up in an attempt to drag it away. That too was destroyed and set on fire. Joe May of No. 1 Platoon played his part in this, using the two-inch mortar.

There was a supply drop during the afternoon which attracted a lot of flak, but some of which fell in the Company positions. The close presence of anti-aircraft guns caused rear-gunners of the Stirlings flying this mission to fire on ground positions. This was quite understandable but had unfortunate results for some. Arthur Heath in his slit trench alongside Sergeant Kent was one who was wounded in this way.

Bill Mollett, who seems to have been very observant, noted for that day something of which the War Diary makes no mention. Yet General Urquhart's account bears out Mollett's note: 'Can hear our own artillery on the other side of the river very plainly now.' It was the first evidence the Company would have that 30 Corps was nearby. If the gunners were that close, could the tanks be far away? General Urquhart mentions ' . . . contact with outside artillery by radio. . . . select targets for the 64th Medium Regiment when it got in range' on this day. Soon, at a distance of 11 miles, the mediums were ranging in on nominated targets 'some no more than one hundred yards from the perimeter's edge.'

As the General says, there is no more terrifying noise in war than the whine and tremendous blast of these medium shells. The gunners seem to have broken up several German attacks supported by SP guns on the eastern flank.

The perimeter defence had been assigned to the two Brigadiers, Hicks and Hackett, at the morning's Divisional conference. Hicks was given command of the west and the north with the remains of three companies of the Border Regiment (west), the 21st Independent Parachute Company which (with mixed forces of Poles, Glider Pilots and Royal Engineers) took on what would normally be reckoned a battalion frontage in the north-west corner and the remains of the battalion of the KOSB on the northern edge.

It was on the KOSB's front that the Germans pressed home the most determined attack of the day and the artillery did not stop it. The Company War Diary refers to this: 'During the afternoon the KOSBs on our right flank were heavily attacked and forced from their position. This was later re-established.' Bill Mollett writes: 'The KOSBs filtered through our lines again and we finally got orders to turn them back and shoot if they refused.' A great deal lies behind the War Diary's words that the position 'was later re-established.' The impression in the Company was that the KOSBs broke and ran. Some of them actually penetrated No. 3 Platoon's position and got as far as Company HQ before they were turned back. General Urquhart explains:

' . . . the KOSBs, who had previously been subjected to intense mortaring, had to halt the Germans with the bayonet. They re-occupied their positions only at high cost and in the end were reduced to 150 all ranks.' You can only 're-occupy' a position if you have been driven from it. The fact that they did go back and re-occupy it is in no small measure due to the encouragement given them by the Company on to whose positions they were driven.

The General continues:

'In the heat and haze of battle, the Independent Company got the impression that the KOSBs had been wiped out, and there was some alarm when this report came through'. There was no 'alarm' so far as the Company was concerned! Rather was there concern that this element of the Division had for the moment cracked. But back they did go and one can only think they, the poor old KOSBs, preferred to face the Germans rather than the pathfinders.

General Urquhart takes up the story again: 'What had happened was that the KOSBs had sidestepped a couple of houses to shorten their line. Even now there was a disconcerting stretch of open ground between them and the Independent Company. The line of houses was not continuous and the KOSBs were in a somewhat dangerous spot.' It was some side-step – right into the Company lines and it was the 'disconcerting stretch of open ground' filled with retreating KOSBs which concerned No. 3 Platoon. Anyway, the lapse was easily forgiven – if not forgotten.

Another item which escaped the attention of the Company diarist was the visit of the Divisional commander. Mollett did not miss it. Neither did Phil Eden of No. 3 Platoon who was wounded that day. He recalls the General jumping from his jeep, diving in a slit trench and asking for his map case and papers to be recovered. 'A few tried, but armoured vehicles had the Jeep covered.' For Phil Eden that day led to seven months in a German Stalag.

It is typical of the limited view point each man had that Bill Mollett saw the General's arrival in a different light. He says: 'In the early evening the Divisional commander suddenly appeared in a Jeep in the field and belted across in the open. Not a shot fired at him.' Others were only vaguely aware of this arrival and the Company diarist certainly does not mention it either on this day or the day before. In the context of his book this visit could have occurred the day before. General Urquhart writes: 'On one of my trips I went up to see Boy Wilson and his Independent Company who held a number of houses in a heavily wooded district.' At that time we occupied only one house, Ommershof. 'I wanted to see how he was doing and also to warn him of Hackett's possible appearance in the Independent Company's area from the north.' At this stage in the battle Hackett was committed to the east and south so that Urquhart might well be speaking of the day before or even the day before that when No. 1 Platoon was out on LZ 'L'.

The General continues: 'Suddenly we found ourselves in the middle of a vigorous dispute between the Independent Company and some SS men. From the slit trenches on the roadside, faces appeared and men shouted and gesticulated. I braked hard and with Roberts, made an undignified dive into a ditch. We had run between the lines: the ride was No Man's Land. As little was to be gained by staying put, I decided to make a run for it to the house occupied by Wilson some fifty yards away on a slightly wooded rise.' This was undoubtedly, 'Ommershof'.

He goes on: 'I told Roberts of my intention and told him to collect the Jeep, if he could. We ventured out simultaneously. I reached the house without being molested, but Roberts attracted some enemy attention when he climbed into the Jeep. The ride was too narrow to allow him to turn round. So he decided to drive on towards the right-hand turn which looped round close to the house. Going fast, he negotiated the corner and swerved to avoid a burned-out German half-track.' Probably, Landon's SP gun. 'Something must have hit the Jeep,' Urquhart writes, 'for the steering suddenly collapsed. Roberts was thrown clear and rolled into a ditch. He shook himself and heard disembodied voices calling advice. From the undergrowth around him came the call: 'For God's sake get out of it! Sniper!' He had a severe pain in his leg but in desperation he managed to jump over a four-and-a-half feet high wire-mesh fence. When he arrived at the house, he had a large swelling on his forehead as well as a leg injury and I sent him off to the RAP (Regimental Aid Post) for treatment. More than anything he was worried about my jeep. ' "I'm afraid, sir," he said sadly, "that it's a complete write-off." '

It seems highly likely that this all took place that day (as both Mollett and Eden recall it) and not the day before because it was that night that the General decided to reduce the perimeter, particularly in view of what had happened to the KOSBs. 'I therefore decided', he says, 'to pull back the KOSBs a few houses, brought over the Recce Squadron with the Independent Company and a squadron of Sappers to the eastern side of Hackett and formed the Divisional RASC into a small force which went into the line between Boy Wilson's men and Lonsdale Force.'

The Divisional commander signalled south: 'No knowledge elements of the Division in Arnhem for 24 hours.' In other words, he did not know whether or not Frost still held the bridge. 'Balance of Division in very tight perimeter. Heavy mortaring and machine gun fire followed by local attacks. Main nuisance SP guns. Our casualties heavy. Resources stretched to the utmost. Relief within 24 hours vital.' That was on Thursday 21 September. The men of Oosterbeek had far more than 24 hours still to endure.

The Company War Diary says: 'Orders were received to withdraw to a position in the 4th Parachute Brigade area under whose command we were to be. Area is called "Hartestein".'

On this day at 17.15 hours the Polish Parachute Brigade had dropped south of the river near Driel in face of stiff German resistance and without the assistance of the pathfinders.

Friday 22 September, the sixth day of the action, began for the Company at 01.00 hours when it formed up in the grounds of Ommershof ready to move off. One man was reluctant to leave the comparative safety of his foxhole and had to be encouraged out of it with his section sergeant's Colt automatic in his ear. There were few signs of lack of courage in the pathfinder Company. When they did show, it came with a sense of shock to those who observed them. General Urquhart shows a good understanding of the problem, which so far as the Company was concerned was minimal. It did, however, manifest itself in one serious case, but this is not the place to discuss it.

The Company moved off. It was a pitch-dark night and in order to maintain contact each man had to hold on to the tail of the parachutist's camouflaged smock of the man in front. The move was made with great caution and with the minimum of noise. The Company was still the coherent force it had always been. It knew not quite where it might find itself at dawn nor what the day ahead might bring. For some, it brought death; for others, wounds and captivity; still others, survived and gained MMs, MCs, DCMs, and DSOs. Some were to earn, but not receive, VCs.

Joe May of No. 1 Platoon disappeared that night. No one knew what happened to him or how he met his end. He was present in the grounds of Ommershof when his sergeant checked his section. He was absent next morning when the same sergeant checked his men into position under the trees near the Hartenstein Hotel. It was easy to go astray if contact was lost in the dark. Still, Joe's disappearance remains a mystery. No shots were fired that night and so far as is known, no contact was made with the enemy. Years later, Joe May's section commander, revisiting Oosterbeek, came across his grave in the Airborne Cemetery. To this day he has no idea as to how Joe died and it is probable that he never will.

The Company War Diary for September 22 reads:
'02.30 hours. The Company were successfully withdrawn without opposition and rested by 4th Parachute Brigade HQ for the night.
05.00 hours. The Company took up their new positions in houses in the Eastern perimeter between the two CCS. Apart from mortar fire the enemy appeared to be unaware of our position and no attack developed.'

No. 1 Platoon crossed to the north of the main Utrecht-Arnhem road and entered houses on Station Weg including the one on the north-west corner of the cross roads opposite the CCS (Casualty Clearing Station) on the north-east corner and diagonally opposite the Schöonoord Hotel on the south-east side of the crossroads. The rest of the Company remained to the south of the main road and the platoons took up positions in houses in the Paasberg and Peitersberge Roads. Company HQ was established in a doctor's house with its garden forming the apex of the triangular junction of the two roads.

The Schöonoord was being used as a CCS as well as the Hotel Vreewijk opposite. These two buildings under the protection of the Red Cross were to give the Company some trouble in the days to follow. They provided a covered approach to the Company's positions which the Germans were not slow to make use of. When they both fell into German hands later it was galling for survivors in the houses on the other side of the street to see their wounded comrades taken into the casualty clearing stations where they automatically became prisoners of war. It was tantalizing to see Germans in the grounds moving freely in and about the buildings and if they wore Red Cross armbands not to be able to shoot them. But no mercy was shown to anyone who appeared without such protection.

Most of the Company now had a roof over their heads for the first time since the action began. They also had daily contact with civilians, for most of the houses had cellars where the local population hid for days on end, only coming up for a blow of fresh air after dark.

The platoons settled down to make their new 'homes' as battle worthy as possible. Some with suitable front gardens had men dig in outside under hedgerows. In most cases, however, in order to gain a better field of fire ground floor windows were ignored, shutters closed and front doors locked and bolted, a sentry placed on the back door; then the first floor frontage was prepared as a Bren gun position, with all glass shattered and removed and furniture and bedding wedged in the window frames as some sort of cover behind which to operate. Snipers and other riflemen were put into roof attics, front and rear.

German snipers also operated from vantage points in concealed positions both in front and behind the houses. To go outside was always precarious in daylight. A bullet might be expected from almost any direction. If it can be said that there was a front, it was the street outside the front door and in many cases the enemy were the immediate neighbours in and around the houses opposite.

It was, however, a relief and a novelty to be inside a house again and to see and talk to civilians. It rained that morning. And it rained mortar bombs, which accounted for some casualties in outside positions. Max Rodley was one of them. Killed in his slit trench. Only that morning he had posed for a photograph taken by a Dutch lady in a group consisting of Sergeant Binick, Ben Swallow, Paddy Cameron, Jock McCausland, Mitchell and Jefferies. Two glider pilots are also in the group. Before the next two days were ended both Rodley and Cameron would be dead, Ben Swallow, Mitchell and Sergeant Binick wounded and Ben would die of his wounds in German hands at Apeldoorn in the following months.

The Company's casualty rate increased considerably after moving into the houses. Patrols were sent out in the afternoon and the War Diary notes:

'16.00 hours. Two patrols were sent out, one from No. 3 Platoon and one from No. 2 Platoon. The object being (a) to try and contact 10th Parachute Battalion east of our position and (b) to try and push our line further out. Both patrols came under heavy MG fire and contact could not be made with 10th Battalion. Casualties 1 killed and 2 wounded. It appears that the enemy are well dug into strong points about 400 yards to our front.'

Tommy Scullion of No. 2 Platoon remembers that patrol in which he was No. 2 on the Bren. His No. 1 was tough little Private J. V. Fiely who, Tommy says, ' . . . at a corner went down with his head blown off by a Spandau.' Peter Holt was also on that patrol and testifies to the shattering effect of this MG fire.

The remnants of 10th Parachute Battalion were holding out in houses along the main road east of the crossroads in a position which was becoming more and more isolated as it stuck out from the edge of the perimeter like a sore thumb. It was a position which could not be held much longer against the growing enemy strength, which included a number of half-tracked SP guns. These prowled around the whole eastern sector, appearing now here, now there. It seemed that every house the Company occupied received one or more shells from these guns during the day.

Most of the men were by now down to eating their emergency ration, a golden tin of hard concentrated chocolate. From the cellars, jars of preserved fruit and jam were taken sparingly with whatever remained of the hard biscuits. The water situation was desperate since the Germans had cut off the supply. It was a grim first day in the houses of Oosterbeek, but worse were to follow.

It rained that night, but it was relatively quiet. The men not on watch or patrol got some much needed sleep under cover for a change. Put together, the Company's casualties equalled the total of the previous five days. In other words, they had doubled in that 24 hours. Amongst them was Alan Sharman, who had received his third wound of the war. Under cover of smoke, he and his platoon were busy driving the enemy from a house near the school in Paasberg Weg. He was attended by the diminutive Italian medical orderly, Gambadella, and eventually found himself once more in a German-held CCS and a POW for the third time.

It was drizzling when Saturday 23 September dawned, but long before that dawn No. 3 Platoon, under Lieutenant Ashmore and Sergeant Smith, had moved out to relieve the 10th Battalion in its 'sore thumb' position. This began a grim day for the whole Company.

The War Diary reads: '03.00 hours – 3 Platoon moved up and took up the positions occupied by 10th Battalion who were withdrawn into reserve. This position is very isolated and I objected to occupying it. The Brigadier, however, insisted as it protects the CCS.' Later: '07.30 hours. 3 Platoon position is heavily attacked with 1 Mark IV tank and two SP guns supporting infantry.'

1 Platoon received the overflow of this attack. Sergeant Jerry Thompson, with the remains of his section, rushed wild-eyed into No. 1 Section's position, without helmet and looking for Germans. He had been blasted out of his house by SP guns on the main road. The house had literally been brought down about their ears. Before leaving, Jerry had hurled a Gammon bomb of his own concoction into a mob of Germans, who in arrogant confidence had entered his garden. Jerry had killed a lot of Germans and now, quite berserk, was looking for more. He was killed soon after and others of his section were badly wounded in 1 Platoon's sector.

One of these was 'Umbriago' Hillier. Already wounded, Hillier went back to help a comrade and was hit again, this time in the throat. When he broke back into 1 Section's beleaguered position it looked to be a fatal wound. 1 Platoon was itself under pressure; phosphorous shells set up a lot of thick white smoke. The position was chaotic as 1 Platoon tried to cover the retreat of the patrol on their front.

Ben Swallow in Hotel Strijland next door to 1 Section drew back the men he had in the grounds into the cover of the hotel. Next door, Ron Kent evacuated the house and prepared to receive an assault by the Germans under cover of the smoke. It never came. The battle died down. No. 1 Section re-occupied the house, which was subsequently burnt to the ground. Ben Swallow, in his fortress hotel, was shot from the rear. He died of this wound over a month later. Ben had been a Lincolnshire man and like Ron Kent, a solicitors' clerk. Highly intelligent, Ben might have followed a distinguished legal career, had he lived.

'Rape' Martin, a fellow-Sergeant and close friend of Jerry Thompson, was also killed that day. 'Paddy' Cockings, a sergeant of No. 3 Platoon, was put 'in the bag' along with his section and the 'sore thumb' position which the 10th Battalion had previously held was snuffed out. There was now a hard core defence of Station Weg, held by No. 1 Platoon with glider pilots on their left; the crossroads, at which behind an oak tree, Private Avalon operating a Bren gun of No. 1 Platoon had died.

According to the Company Diary No. 3 Platoon had 15 casualties that day. One SP gun was destroyed. Mollett says this was by No. 2 Platoon's cook, using his PIAT. In No. 1 Platoon, Private Avalon, before he died, is given credit for having destroyed an enemy truck on the main road. It was full of ammunition, caught fire and blew up.

A motor cycle and sidecar was also shot up. With Platoon HQ in the corner house commanding a limited view down the road into Arnhem, Private Alfred ('Ginger') Jones heard the combination arrive at the house next door and witnessed the officer get out and make for the house. 'We watched open-mouthed. Then we all woke up and opened fire.' Both officer and driver were hit. They were later collected by a medical officer and taken into the CCS across the road.

Amidst all the chaos and confusion the medics, protected by nothing but their Red Cross arm-bands, were seen throughout the day coming and going with wounded to the CCS, crossing and re-crossing roads which were frequently under mortar fire and which for the fighting man were covered by MG and sniper fire. Both sides, however, were careful not to fire on the Red Cross and in the main the medics were able to go about their unenviable errands of mercy unmolested. They showed a special kind of courage and were much admired by the men who watched them.

It was one of the tragedies of the action that the CCS's were now in German hands. Any man entering there would automatically become a prisoner of war. This did not deter Company Sergeant Major Jim Stewart from penetrating one of them to see for himself how things were going for the wounded and to have a word of cheer with them. On sandalled feet he passed through No. 1 Platoon's lines, visited the CCS and slipped out again under the German sentries' noses to re-appear again in No. 1 Platoon's position.

During this day, General Urquhart says that typical of the spirit of the Division was the Independent Company. Under Wilson, they had, in the new position into which they had been moved, continued their task of spreading alarm among the Wehrmacht. 'At sniping they were even more formidable than the enemy. Concealed in positions around the Hotel Schoonhord the dressing station which the enemy had taken, they now proceeded to pick off the German sentries. In a raid, some of Wilson's men kidnapped three Germans from behind their own lines and soon afterwards a voice came up on the radio telephone saying, "You must let our boys go. Otherwise we'll come and take your Sunray." Sunray was the code name for the Divisional Commander. Wilson chuckled into the microphone: "Come and get him if you can." '

Boy Wilson personified the character of the Company he led and, as General Urquhart recalls, 'paid regular evening visits to Divisional HQ at the Hartenstein to "cheer them up at Division" with amusing tales of his Company's adventures. He always gave the impression that his men were very happy where they were on the eastern edge of the perimeter.'

At the river the Poles were still trying to get across and a few had succeeded. These 35 were taken under command by Brigadier Hicks on the western perimeter. Many had drowned in the attempt and by first light on Sunday no more than 50 had got across. Later, some 200 Poles succeeded in making the crossing and the Divisional commander talked with Lieutenant Colonel Loder-Symonds and Major Wilson and agreed to let Brigadier Hackett's eastern perimeter have the first body of Poles as reinforcements.

The Company War Diary for Sunday 24 September opens: 'By first light it was seen that the enemy occupied the CCS at the crossroads between 3 Platoon and 1 Platoon and a considerable amount of sniping came from this area. The enemy further infiltrated behind No. 1 Platoon's position from their left (northern) flank and snipers were active. A number of snipers were killed during the day.'

Mollett, who incidentally in his diary ran the events of this day and the previous one together (just as did Sergeant Kent, who had run Wednesday and Thursday together in his recollections and thus thought that this day's events occurred on Saturday), speaks of heavy mortaring and particularly the attention of about 'four 88s's'. These are also mentioned in the Company War Diary which continues:

'They also started to set fire to houses with phosphorous bombs. A heavy attack was launched to the right of our front, which was partially successful and some enemy endeavoured to infiltrate into our positions but were destroyed. In spite of the continuous shelling and mortar fire to which the Company had been subjected for five days and nights, making rest almost impossible, their spirits were at a high level and there was no thought of submission.

'At about 11.00 hours,' the Diary continues, 'No. 1 Platoon reported some Polish paratroops in their area and at 12.00 hours they relieved No. 1 Platoon, who stood down for a rest.' The arrival of the Poles in No. 1 Platoon's position was quite unexpected. Mollett says 'Movements in the house next door (held by Sergeant Kent's No. 1 Section) and realise it's the advance guard of the Poles.' Kent, who thought this was Saturday, noted that ' . . . the chatter of many voices, sounding very like German, sent me scuttling downstairs with my Sten gun at the ready.'

The Poles tended to stand around in large groups quite oblivious of the danger from snipers and took about ten casualties in this way in as many minutes. They were eventually persuaded into the houses and No. 1 Platoon handed over their positions and were told to rest as best they could in downstair backrooms.

Mollett puts the wounding of Sergeant Ben Swallow, which led to his death, as taking place after the arrival of the Poles. It may well have been, but Sergeant Kent in the house next door was aware of it as he made the final rounds of the house he had occupied with his section since Friday morning and still thinks it happened on Saturday. Such is the confusion of an action of this nature.

'At 15.00 hours No. 2 Platoon reported considerable enemy movement on their right flank and it was clear that the enemy

were bent on seizing the CCS situated on the right of No. 2
Platoon.' This would be Hotel Tafelberg.

The War Diary goes on:

'This had previously been held by some glider pilots who had
been removed at the request of the Germans so as not to
endanger the wounded in the CCS. It appeared at one time as if
the enemy attack would swing round the back of our position. I
therefore moved No. 1 Platoon, who were resting, to the HQ
area in close support. However, having gained possession of the
CCS, the enemy made no further move.'

No. 1 Platoon's move from its Station Weg positions to
Company HQ was carried out under cover of smoke across the
main road. It was a hectic mad dash, the whole Platoon electing
to run the gauntlet together, which were the right tactics in the
bullet-swept situation. Only one slight casualty was sustained:
Tommy McMahon, that irrepressible humorist, was hit in the
foot by the odd bullet. He was soon joking about it, in
characteristic fashion, saying that if he was an American he
could claim a Purple Heart!

The Company War Diary then says: 'No. 1 Platoon took over
a part of No. 3 Platoon's line both platoons being down to a
rather low level in numbers. This considerably helped to
consolidate our position which was strengthened by eight glider
pilots with a Bren gun.'

Most of No. 1 Platoon had been able to have a couple of
hours' rest, but the senior NCOs had to reconnoitre the positions
they were to take over. At Company HQ it was good to see
friendly faces one had not expected to see again. A small
thing, but one which deserves recording, if only to show the
kind of comradeship which existed in the Company occurred
here. Ron Kent, an inveterate pipe-smoker, met his close pal,
Sergeant 'Slim' Summerville, in Doctor van Maanen's house
and was presented with a perfectly good briar pipe. 'I've been
keeping it for you', said 'Slim'. Ron, who was smoking the
stump of his last remaining pipe, accepted it gratefully. He had
come into the action with three pipes and half a pound of
tobacco stuffed into his pudding basin helmet. He still had
tobacco and matches, but his last pipe had a broken stem. He
was overjoyed to continue the action, and come out of it, with a
pipe clamped between his teeth.

During the afternoon a truce of sorts had been arranged and
the wounded were moved up the road from the Tafelberg Hotel
to the crossroads CCS under the tired, watchful eyes of the

Company. It was a melancholy sight. Earlier, as the Company War Diary records:

'... two Mark IV tanks were reported in front of No. 3 Platoon. Later a message was received via one of our MO's to the effect that unless I agreed to vacate a house some 30 yards from the CCS at once the German Commander would send two tanks against my position and blast me out.' Major Wilson did not take kindly to this threat. The house was, he considered, vital to the Company's position. He passed a message back to say that he would only agree to this if the Germans would withdraw from the vicinity of the CCS and take their tanks back at least a mile, and undertake not to make any advance in the area of the CCS until all casualties were cleared. 'To add colour to the threat', the Diary records, 'Private Dixon, No. 3 Platoon ACC cook, sneaked out with his PIAT and destroyed one of the tanks.' The PIAT bomb struck the back of the tank and set off some ammunition. The other tank moved back and enemy troops in the vicinity of the CCS withdrew.

No. 1 Platoon moved into the small school on the east side of the street called Paasberg. This was the Company's most advanced position commanding a field of fire of 50 to 100 yards to the houses and the backs of houses on Anna Straat. Sergeants Stan Sullivan and Ron Kent were in charge. What was left of two sections went into the school under cover of darkness and by way of the windows facing on to the street. The regular entrance was too exposed to sniper fire and illuminated with fires burning in the area.

Platoon HQ and the rest of the platoon occupied houses in the street to the rear. A much depleted No. 3 Platoon held other houses nearby, and No. 2 Platoon yet others to the south towards the Tafelberg Hotel. The school had been used as an RAP earlier in the battle and six corpses almost a week old occupied a classroom needed as a Bren gun position. The smell of death hung heavy in the air and there was blood, dried and stinking, everywhere. Bloody bandages and toilet paper used as bandages littered the floor. One of the first jobs was to remove the bodies to a back room and to clean up the floor. This was done and the Bren gun sited. At a small circular window near the entrance Sid Humphries, a sharp shooter, placed himself to watch a small sector of the front.

There was not much left to do that night but maintain watch. Regular watches were arranged for the night and Ron Kent, having handed over to Stan Sullivan for a couple of hours, was taking a rest when he was aroused to go to Company HQ. David Eastwood was out on patrol and Platoon Sergeant Binick wounded by mortar splinters, so Kent thought the CO had orders for the platoon. Not so – they were orders for him. Alone, he was to make his way back to No. 1 Platoon's old position and deliver a message to the Polish commander and a battery for his radio. Across the main road and into the backs of the houses on Station Weg, careful contact with the trigger-happy Poles, into the Hotel Strijland, previously occupied by Ben Swallow and his section, delivery of message and wireless battery and back again, took best part of one and a half careful hours. The distance covered was negligible and in normal circumstances would not have taken 15 minutes.

It is typical of the reaction of brain fatigue which most men suffered that Kent thought this happened on Saturday/Sunday whereas it was the night of Sunday/Monday. He had somehow run the events of Wednesday and Thursday together and thus lost a day. In the same way Mollett in his diary ran Friday and Saturday together. The Company diarist is probably the only one who, through all the Company endured, was able to clearly distinguish one day from another. Most of the men were talking in terms of 'the day we brought in the Poles', 'the day Fiely was killed' or 'the day we moved into the houses'. They did not know whether it was Monday, Tuesday or Friday, nor did they much care for such fine distinctions. They cared about helping each other, staying put, sticking it out to the end. There was a noticeable tendency to show one another particular consideration. There was no friction, no 'bitching', no cry of 'that's not my job': true comradeship which so many were to miss on return to civilian life. This, in spite of the fact that most of them were nearing the end of endurance, though they would not admit it.

At some stage during these days in the houses Major Wilson had been worried about the state of the Bren guns. They had certainly been overworked and he was afraid that the barrels would wear out (each gun had a spare barrel) and that the gas valves would become corroded with accumulated residues. He pays tribute to Sergeant 'Nick' Carter, REME, the armourer, who constantly went around checking the guns and putting them right. A lot of the trouble was due to dust from shattered buildings and recoil springs had to be cleaned frequently. Most of the Bren gunners and their NCO's were careful to take good care of their guns, however.

Unknown to the Company, things were happening which pointed to the end of their ordeal. The perimeter had shrunk. Here and there a hundred yards had to be given up, but none on the Company's sector. The Germans were now calling the perimeter 'Die Hexen Kessel' – the Witches' Cauldron.

On Sunday night, in Nijmegen, Lieutenant General 'Boy' Browning decided that it was time to withdraw the 1st Division, and went off to see General Horrocks. Dempsey of 2nd Army agreed, said 'No' to Horrocks' plan to attempt a crossing further to the west. 'Get them out', Dempsey said and turning to Browning, 'Is that alright with you?' Montgomery had promptly concurred, although it meant the end of his plan to break into the north of Germany and send his armour rolling down into enemy country, and would thus postpone the end of the war in Europe until the following year.

It was the right decision, but it was not taken in time to prevent an attempt on the night of the 24/25 September to lodge 250 of the 4th Battalion of the Dorsetshire Regiment on the north bank of the Neder Rijn. Those of the Dorsets who were not killed were captured.

None of this made any impact on the Company, who were unconscious of the efforts being made to reach them. So far as they were concerned, they were there to stay until there was nothing left with which to fight or until the 2nd Army relieved them.

It is relevant here to mention what General Urquhart has observed about the individual will to resist. 'In some cases', he says, 'it was instinctive resistance. In others, the last instalments of will power were dredged. There were some who were "bomb happy" – to whom nothing mattered anymore.' There were instances in which the nerves of men had broken, their resistance and self-control snapped and who could no longer think straight. There were those whom no inducement could make come out of the cellars and face the constant barrage as others were doing. 'I am sure', Urquhart writes, 'that the will-power and courage required in battle are very different to the quality commonly called "guts" when it is related to such sports as horse-riding and boxing. Contact with the enemy means that men are up against, not so much an obvious, visual problem as, the unknown, the unexpected and the unsuspected. It is their will-power or character which counts and, as Lord Moran once wrote, the main essential is to have control of one's will-power and that is a question of conscience which comes back to character.'

The 21st Independent Parachute Company was possessed of a large measure of this quality and this pays high tribute to those judges of character who selected them, John Lander and Bob Wilson.

Monday 25 September – the ninth day – started no differently from any of the past few days. After a quiet uneventful night shelling and mortaring started up at a very reasonable hour. One gained the impression that the enemy observed a working day and then cleared off and went to bed. 'The left flank remained quiet during the morning, but the whole Company front was submitted to heavy bombardment and an increasing number of light phosphorous mortar bombs were fired. More houses caught fire as a result. The enemy made an unsuccessful attempt to infiltrate into the right of our position, which cost him casualties, and an attack on our left in the afternoon was driven off.'

No. 2 Platoon were most concerned with the right flank, but No. 1 Platoon's Bren gun in the school was kept busy. Riflemen kept their weather-eye open, but fired only when sure of a target. At one stage, seeing a German in Anna Straat but out of range of his Sten gun, No. 1 Section sergeant nudged Sid Humphries, 'Get him.' Sid Humphries 'got him' and as the man fell he spun and showed, on his right arm hitherto concealed, a Red Cross. For a second Sid and the sergeant looked at each other. Then Sid said in his slow country accent, 'Well, he asked for it – standing in the open like that.' It was as if he regretted the German's lack of expertise; as if he resented the suggestion that the German had shown contempt for his (Sid's) personal marksmanship. All this was expressed in his few words and the look he gave his sergeant, the man who had accidentally shot him below the knee in Italy. Neither of them would forget that, but no resentment flowed from that incident either. Sid Humphries was one of those whom St. Paul would have described as 'the salt of the earth'. He was typical of all that was best in the Company. Solid, reliable, not given to emotional outbursts; he served; did his job with commendable quiet efficiency. He was one of the originals.

At 16.00 hours the Company War Diary records: 'A conference was held at Divisional HQ at which orders to withdraw over the river that night were given. The Independent Company were to form the rearguard arriving at the river at 22.30 hours.' Two hours later a Company 'O' Group was called at which orders were issued to cover the forming up of the Company along a wood, later vacated by 4th Parachute Brigade. No. 1 Platoon was to be head of the column. The Company was to be in position ready to move at 21.45 hours. Every precaution was to be taken against making any noise during the move. These orders were passed on to the platoons by their commanders shortly after the 'O' Group broke up. The news was received with mixed feelings. No one had thought of a withdrawal. They expected to be relieved by 2nd Army or to remain where they were until lack of ammunition or life itself deprived them of the ability to resist any more. They, the great nameless 'they', would not have expressed it in quite that way, but that is what it amounts to.

Between 18.00 hours when the 'O' Group was held at Company HQ and 19.00 hours, the word went around the platoon positions. 'We're getting out across the river tonight. Get your boots covered with strips of blanket and see that none of your equipment is loose or rattles. We move out by sections starting at 21.25 hours. Assemble in the open patch behind the wood near 4th Brigade HQ. Company will act as rearguard and move off at 21.45 hours – No. 1 Platoon leading. Glider pilots are taping a route down to the part of the river where Canadian REs will have some boats to take us across. A pair of Bofors will be firing two streams of red tracer at intervals from about 21.30 hours onwards. They will give you some indication of the direction to head for if you go astray. Any questions?'

The Company Diary takes up the story of the Company's last few hours in The Cauldron: 'At approximately 21.00 hours 30 Corps artillery opened up a terrific bombardment on a wood which was occupied by the enemy just south of our position and through which we were to pass. This bombardment was answered by the enemy who at 21.15 hours put down everything he had into the area, making the forming up of the Company very difficult and hazardous. To add to the difficulties the enemy set fire to almost all the houses we were occupying.'

In the houses and the school, the men waited nervously for the order to move out. Nervously, because with deliverance now so close to hand everyone was acutely conscious of the danger of being killed or wounded at the last minute. This danger had always been there but was accepted as a matter of course all the time they were expected to stay and fight. Though the thought was hardly expressed, everyone felt what bloody bad luck it would be to stop a bullet or chunk of mortar or shell at this stage.

In the school, Stan Sullivan passed the last few minutes of waiting writing on a blackboard a message intended to encourage the Dutch who might see it and to show the Germans our defiance. 'WE'LL BE BACK' he wrote. Shortly after, it was time to move. One at a time men left their positions and took up their places in single file, well spaced out and made their way like silent, shadowy ghosts into the night. Moving from cover to cover, shadow to shadow, in a night lit only by the fires from the burning houses. The scene was like an illustration for Dante's *Inferno*, with the crashing explosion of shells from 30 Corps perilously close to the fringes of the perimeter and the flash and bursting of mortar bombs within it.

According to the War Diary it was 22.00 before the Company moved off from the 'forming up point'. Most of the men had lain in the mud and rain of the cabbage patch which was the FUP for more than half an hour and some from sheer weariness may have dropped off to sleep. A link in the chain was broken, with the result that half the Company moved off and left part of No. 1 Platoon and Sergeant Dick Wilkins' platoon still lying in the mud. As the minutes ticked by he and Ron Kent began to move along the line to find out what was happening. They met and decided they had better move the men out themselves. There was no officer present. They had evidently gone with Company HQ and the rest of the Company. It was a pitch dark night and raining hard. The men made no sound that could possibly be heard above the roar of the guns and the explosion of shells and mortar bombs. Everything favoured a silent undetected escape.

The men left behind were fortunate. They found and followed the white tape put down by the glider pilots and though it was a slow, groping, 'stop-start' business they reached the riverside road, near which a gas works was burning, at about 23.30 hours. Over to the left of the course they had taken the rest of the Company were not faring so well.

'It was now raining hard and the enemy guns and mortars were a little quieter' says the Company War Diary. 'Two halts had been made so as to keep the Company closed up, when at approximately 22.30 hours, whilst proceeding through the wood recently shelled by our artillery, the head of the column was halted by a German MG post which immediately opened fire with at least two LMGs. The CO and one officer at the head of the column became casualties and part of the leading section. Little confusion was caused, however, and enemy shooting became wild when '36' grenades were thrown back at them. The

2 I/C (Captain R. E. Spivey) reformed the Company and taking a right-hand sweep reached the river with the majority of the Company and crossed to the south bank where the CO later rejoined, being only slightly injured by a bullet grazing his nose and right eye.'

The CO had had an amazingly close call, but the officer who had gone down with him, Lieutenant J. Horsley of the Border Regiment who had been attached to the Company for the operation, was dead. It was during this episode that C.S.M. Stewart won his DCM.

For the next few hours the Company, now in its two separate segments, lay out in the soaking meadowland which bordered the river, awaiting their turn to enter the all-too-few canvas-sided, collapsible assault boats manned by the Canadians. All through the night these brave fellows made the journey to and fro, from one bank to the other of the fast-flowing river which at this point was about 200 yards wide. From time to time MG fire from von Tettau's 9th SS Panzers on the high ground above Heveadorp swept the meadows; everyone 'froze' like statues under the light of parachute flares put up by the enemy; mortar bombs burst around and about the assembled remains of the Division, here and there could be heard the moans of the walking wounded and the sudden cries of the newly stricken. For most it was a wait of at least two agonised hours, for others it was as much as four. Some, like Ken 'Darkie' Roberts, decided to give up a place in a boat and swim for it. Fine athlete and strong swimmer though he was, he died in the attempt. Many others were lost that night. Some there were who at dawn were still on the river's edge unable to cross, the boats having ceased to operate as during the night the small number had been diminished by gun fire.

On the other side, still in the dark of the night, the Company was for the first time in all that action no longer a cohesive force. They had come across as and how they could, although one section at least, or what was left of it, had managed to stay together for the river crossing. Once over, however, it was very much every man for himself. Each would make his way, at the pace which suited him, south; first to Driel, where the Poles had been fighting and on to Elst. They arrived at these places at widely spaced intervals. Here and there one would come across a member of the Company and then move on either singly or in twos and threes. Any attempt at regimentation at that stage would have been not only foolhardy but impossible.

Some, like Bill Mollett stopped to rest near the positions of units of 30 Corps alongside the road. Others marched on through the night, silent and grim, thinking of another retreat – the one to Dunkirk – and resenting it and at the same time regretting the comrades left behind, dead, wounded or missing and the bitter disappointment of the Dutch whose hopes of seeing the last of the Germans were now shattered.

From dawn onwards through the morning of Tuesday 26 September, the men of the Company began to arrive in Nijmegen by whatever transport they could find. At Elst there was quite a fleet of ambulances and many were brought into Nijmegen as casualties under the protection of the Red Cross. In Nijmegen they were greeted by the Division's seaborne element. As they came in, their names, numbers, rank and unit were noted. They were told to dump all equipment, but many clung to their personal weapons which they had carried throughout the past nine days.

Without a moment's delay, men were led into mess halls previously occupied by the enemy (for Nijmegen had substantial regular Army barracks) and were treated to a sumptuous meal. 'Just like Christmas', one of them remarked. Tea, brandy and cigarettes were served with the meal and there was no queuing. Whoever prepared the reception of the battle's survivors was indeed thoughtful, but this was only part of the story. Every man through whose hands the battle-weary passed showed a consideration and understanding of what their guests had endured.

No attempt was made at this stage to sort men into units. As soon as they had eaten the men were led (not marched) to barracks nearby, where bedding had already been laid out ready for them to fall into. They were simply told: 'Get your heads down, lads, and have a good sleep. There are showers available down the hall when you feel ready for them.' Most just stripped off and slept through the afternoon before showering and shaving. It was noticeable that many slept with their weapons under their blankets and ready to hand. Habits acquired over the days of trial die hard.

Late in the afternoon a parade was called. In the grounds of the barracks NCOs called men to their various unit assembly points. Gradually each man found his place, and platoons and sections reassembled, albeit depleted, under their sergeants and corporals. Officers again took command of their platoons.

Seaborne baggage, kitbags and sleeping-bags were collected and fresh barrack rooms allotted for the night.

Now was the time for renewing acquaintances – some had not seen each other since leaving England – and exchanging news of what had befallen absent comrades. There were stories of remarkable escapes and incidents, some of which were hardly credible unless experienced at first hand. One of these concerned Private Johnny Melford, who appeared dimple-cheeked. He'd never had dimples before. Now he had a neat black hole in each cheek. He happened to be yawning at the moment a bullet chose to hit him in the face! It passed through both cheeks. Had his mouth been closed it is certain that it would have struck bone and teeth and sent the bullet ricocheting around his skull, and Johnny Melford would have known no more.

Talking of 'skulls', Sergeant Gordon 'Slim' Summerville had an endearing habit of referring to the men under his command as 'skulls'. 'Right', he would say to his junior NCOs, 'Get the skulls on parade.' It sounds callous, but it was never intended to be and 'Slim' had as much care and consideration for his men as any of his fellow sergeants. Cleaned up and with a change of clothing from the kitbags, there began the compiling of the casualty lists, each man contributing what he knew of the fate of the absent.

It eventually emerged that the Company had lost one officer and 11 men killed, 24 known to be wounded and assumed prisoner of war, and 29 others missing and assumed prisoner; a total of 65 out of the original 186 all ranks. This was a little more than one third of those who had left England ten days before: a lower ratio than most units could show. Taking the Division as a whole, only one man in four of those who crossed the Lower Rhine escaped to Nijmegen. Within the Company two men out of three had made it.

Much of this can be attributed to the fact that, in spite of the tasks which had taken the platoons in the first few days of the action to widely distributed venues, the Company had never lost its cohesion and identity. It had fought throughout as a unit and had held together well in all circumstances. It had not, it is true, had to play the attacking role of the big battalions and there is no doubt whatsoever that it was in their efforts to reach the bridge that the battalions had sustained their heavy casualties. Even so, the Company had had its full share of exposure on the DZs and LZs and as defenders of the perimeter they had proved their worth against superior firepower and as a unit were not defeated. It says much for the calibre of the pathfinders and of their leaders right down to the most junior NCO that they emerged from the action in the numbers and order they did.

All was not yet over. There were air raids that night and a few showed the strain they had been under. There was also the gauntlet of the 'Corridor' to be run next day. This the Company learned from General Browning, who addressed the remnants of his once élite 1st Airborne Division that evening. Any thought there may have been of putting the Division back into the line was quickly dismissed as soon as it was seen how completely it had been reduced. Loud cheers greeted General Browning's announcement that the survivors would be returning to England as soon as possible.

Newspapers told the Company what an impact the battle had had on the world outside and the same source told of the plans for demobilisation as soon as the war in Europe was ended! Having just emerged from war at its worst, such news seemed premature and unbelievable. The men learned for the first time of the 'Age and Service' system which was to be adopted, but it still seemed all too remote to be taken seriously. It would be a long time yet before some of the younger men would see the end of military service.

It was midday on Wednesday 27 September before the three tonners, carrying the Company in crowded discomfort, rolled southward through Grave, Uden, Veghel, St. Oedenrode, Son, Eindhoven and Valkenwaard and over 'Joe's Bridge' across the Escaut Canal.

Moving down 'the Corridor', the Company saw evidence in plenty of the struggle 30 Corps had had in its attempt to reach the Division. '88s', their long barrels still pointing full of menace straight down the single road, but now silent and incapable of action, were to be seen in plenty. On the road-side were the wrecks and burnt-out hulks of our tanks and troop transports, witnesses to the deadly power of those guns. In the fields were the carcasses of cattle caught up in the carnage and now lying bloated and fly-blown with their legs rigidly pointing skyward. Passing through a small, gutted village where one looked for some life but found none, one cynic remarked, 'I see we well and truly "liberated" this place.'

The road had been cut during the day and the Germans had to be driven off. This had delayed our departure from Nijmegen.

There was another hold up at Veghel where the road was under shell fire. Further delays were caused by the fact that, since priority was always given to traffic heading for the front, the Company transport had to pull off the road to let the more urgent traffic through.

It was late afternoon before the Company reached that ancient seat of learning, Louvain, and evening before billets were found in a large and, what appeared to be, unfinished building connected with the university. Sergeant Gordon and his helpers soon contrived to serve a hot meal of Maconachies' 'M & V' (meat and veg), and since a similar attempt to serve the meal at midday had been frustrated by the sudden order to move, it went down very well. Sleep came easily, even if sleeping bags had to be laid out on bare cement floors in monkish cells lit only by candle light. Hurricane lamps were in short supply and served only the main halls of this strange sanctuary.

The morning of Thursday was spent in speculation as to when the Company would be flying back to England. Packed and only too ready to go the Company yet wondered if they might not enjoy a night out in Brussels! At 15.00 hours the Company moved out of Louvain to a Brussels airfield. Here Dakotas of U.S. Transport Command waited for it to emplane.

The men had a first-class aerial view of Brussels and, though it was in a poor light, the Kentish coast, in the vicinity of Lydd, was easily recognised. The weather deteriorated and the flight seemed to take much longer than the distance merited. Eventually the Company were landed at Saltby, near Grantham, where another splendid meal, beer and cigarettes awaited. It was a wonderful reception and the Company was left in no doubt that it, along with the rest of the Division, were regarded as heroes.

Only now did the men begin to realise their good fortune in coming out of the action, superficially unscathed. Many, however, would carry the mental scars of the past ten days for the rest of their lives. That night the Company returned to its barracks in Newark, which it had left six weeks before when the tentative operations had taken them south into the sealed transit camps. It was a sad return to the old familiar barrack rooms with their all-too-many empty beds.

Newark had become the 'home' of the Company. The first six months of 1944 had been spent chiefly in Lincolnshire. Initially, it had been in the villages of Bassingham, Thirlby and Auborn between Newark and the city of Lincoln. Here the Company had received its replacements after returning from the Central Mediterranean Command. Here these youngsters had trained with the 'veterans'. Yet it was only when the Company as a whole moved into the barracks at Newark that the foundation was laid for its adoption of Newark as its 'home town'.

It was from Newark that the Company set out for its airborne and battle-course exercises on the Yorkshire moors and for the many aborted operations. Now it had 'come home' and for the most part would remain in Newark until the next call came to fly to another country. At that stage of the war none knew where it might be.

The Company's association with Newark and such local institutions as the Church of St. Mary Magdalene, The White Hart and The Ram remain to this day. Many lasting friendships were made in Newark. At least one man married a Newark girl and Tommy Scullion has long since been settled there. The White Hart Inn and The Ram have been the scene of many of the Company's recreational activities. Especially memorable was the night the Company's decorated returned from the Buckingham Palace investiture. The story goes that CSM Jimmy Stewart 'lost' his DCM that night. It remained in the safe keeping of the landlord of the White Hart for quite some time before Jim realised where he had left it.

The awards the Company received as a result of its efforts in Holland were quite remarkable for a unit so small. The CO, Bob Wilson added a DSO to his MC and was promoted to Lieutenant Colonel. David Eastwood and Hugh Ashmore received MCs, Sergeants Binick, Allerton, Smith, Hewitt and Nutter (APTC) eached were awarded MMs. The latter was among the wounded and was a prisoner of war. Fred Lee was awarded the single decoration the Company received from Queen Wilhelmina of the Netherlands.

The 'big picture' (as the lads liked to refer to operation 'Market') was over. Anything that preceded it ranked only as the 'supporting programme' and anything which followed was no more than light entertainment.

Of this operation, Churchill said,' "Not in vain" may be the pride of those who survived and the epitaph of those who fell', while Montgomery's comment was : 'In the years to come it will be a great thing for a man to be able to say "I fought at Arnhem".'

On 27 September 1944 General F. A. M. Browning wrote a personal letter to his old school friend from British Airborne Corps HQ:

'Dear Major Wilson,

I have heard on every side how outstandingly your Company has done. To have earned this special praise from such a gallant body can only mean one thing – that your unit is unsurpassed by any other in the world.

Please tell your chaps what a terrific reputation they have earned.

Yours ever,

Boy Browning'

Perhaps the finest tribute received was from the editorial of the *Daily Mail* which stated quite simply – 'Worthy of their fathers and examples to their sons.' The allusion to the fathers of the men who had fought at Arnhem was most apt, for most of them had fought in the Great War of 1914-18. From what we know of that conflict their ordeals were far worse and more protracted, yet it was pleasing to be identified with such illustrious company.

9 THE INDEPENDENT PLATOON
Greece – Operation 'Manna' and after

It is ironical that the country whose language gave the Western world the word 'democracy' should have been the scene of bitter fighting between that country's people and the troops of a single nation of the Western Powers who were committed to maintaining democracy, as understood by the West.

On return to Italy from the South of France the 1st Independent Parachute Platoon as part of the 2nd Parachute Brigade moved to the neighbourhood of Bari which some of their number had first seen soon after the Company had landed at Taranto in September 1943. Now, a year later, they were to prepare for another operation.

Operation 'Manna' had been on the cards for some time. Its timing depended upon the withdrawal of the Germans from Athens, for it was in Greece that the 2nd Brigade under Brigadier Pritchard was next to see action: action of a kind different to anything they had experienced so far.

During the German occupation of Greece the Greeks had a numerous and very active army of resistance fighters. They made life unpleasant for the Germans along the lonely coast lines and, armed by the Allies from the air, from the mountains. Tragically, the resistance forces themselves split into widely differing factions. Two main forces were involved. The EAM (the National Liberation Front), a broad coalition of liberals, socialists and Communists, but dominated by the Communists because of their superior organisational ability and the fact that

EAM's military arm, the National Popular Army of Liberation (ELAS), was in the main composed of rabid Communists, was by far the stronger. The other main faction was the right wing, pro-West and pro-royalist Greek Democratic League (EDES).

British fears, as expressed by Churchill, were that with the German withdrawal the Communists would impose a left-wing totalitarian regime following the dictates of Stalin's Russia. The Americans did not share this view or did not wish to become involved at that stage. There was some justification for their view because, at one of the three-power wartime conferences, it had been agreed with Soviet Russia that Greece should fall under Britain's sphere of influence while the rest of the Balkans was to be in Russia's. Churchill was more alive to the Communist threat than America wanted to be. The consequence was the bloody conflict which followed.

It was the British intention to support the then constitutional government (the government in exile) until 'the Greek State can be established with a legally armed force and free elections can be held.' It was to this end that British troops were sent into Greece and the reason why the 1st Independent Parachute Platoon as part of 2nd Parachute Brigade next went into what, at first, appeared to be a happy task of liberation and of 'showing the flag' as the parent Company would later do in Norway. Operation 'Manna' began with a company of the 4th Parachute Battalion led by Lieutenant Colonel H. B. Coxen DSO, MC, and accompanied by a section of the pathfinders under Lieutenant 'Dumbo' Willians parachuting onto the airfield at Megara, in a wind of up to 30 miles an hour. With such ground conditions it was inevitable that there were casualties and there were in fact as many as 40, including the medical officer. This was a high percentage of the number dropped. The drop was made at midday on the 12 October, the very day on which high command received confirmation that the Germans were at last pulling out of Athens and withdrawing northward.

The landing was unopposed and the airfield was duly secured in readiness for the descent of the rest of the 2nd Brigade next day. Weather conditions continued to be bad and the arrival of the Brigade was delayed for 24 hours. They and the rest of the Independent Platoon were, in the words of Peter Baker, 'greeted by huge crowds of excited Greeks welcoming their liberators.'

This welcome continued and grew to overwhelming proportions in Athens itself, where the crowds were so thick that the marching troops could not distinguish pavement from street. The Brigadier was apprehensive as he observed that on this hot and thundery day elements in the crowd were getting rough with each other, and one whole battalion was virtually hemmed in by the crowd and having difficulty in proceeding and keeping formation. He called on the chief of police to intervene and disperse the crowds but the police chief declined, believing that such intervention would only incite the crowd the more. He probably knew his fellow countrymen better than did the Brigadier.

The situation appeared to be getting critical when a providential cloudburst drove the people off the streets. The battalions were directed to buildings, selected as being of tactical importance, in and around the city centre.

On the 17/18 October the Brigade was joined by the tanks and men of the 23rd Armoured Brigade which had landed by sea at the Pireaus. Thereafter the British became responsible for policing the city and guarding VPs (vital points), control of which became a matter of dispute with the ELAS guerillas. These last would move in procession through the streets, hindering the movement of the British and making it exceptionally difficult for the Brigade to carry out its task. In soldiers' language they made 'a general bloody nuisance of themselves.' Rival processions would meet and come to blows in the streets, the odd shots were fired, any one of which might have led to a general outbreak of armed warfare. Further such demonstrations were banned. Throughout all this turmoil the parachutists were under strict orders not to become involved, and in spite of rising tension and provocation they rigidly obeyed those orders.

The liberators quickly came to realise that all was not sunshine and flowers. There was poverty and dissension on all sides. Finances were in disorder and food supplies well-nigh exhausted. The troops went on half rations to help feed the civilians. As the Germans steadily withdrew ELAS guerillas moved in to occupy places the Germans left.

Detachments of the 4th Parachute Battalion were sent northward on 17 October and headed for Thebes, 30 miles out of Athens. It became apparent as they advanced that any assistance they thought might be received from the ELAS guerillas would not be forthcoming and that the guerillas regarded them as intruders. This was contrary to the promises their leaders had given the British in the Caserta Agreement. All the ingredients for future trouble were there. It came. Within weeks of the liberators' welcome a large part of the welcomers were in conflict with those they had welcomed.

In the meantime authority decided that an Allied presence was required urgently in Salonika. On 4 November the 5th (Scottish) Parachute Battalion, Brigade HQ and the Independent Parachute Platoon sailed for that port. They were held up by mines in the harbour entrance, but when they landed they were given the same warm welcome they had experienced in Athens. Political tension was, however, apparent and the ELAS guerillas showed no disposition to join in the welcome. News had travelled fast and they realised that 'liberation' by the British did not mean, as they had hoped through all the war years, the handing over of Greece to the Communists. The 5th Scottish pipe-band, by its many parades and performance at trouble spots, helped to distract the populace from political demonstrations and to ease the tension. The drums and pipes accomplished more than any show of force could do.

Later, attached to the 7th Infantry Brigade, the 5th Battalion moved on into Macedonia and Thrace. Brigade HQ and the Independent Platoon flew back to Rome and part of the Brigade returned to Italy to prepare for operations in Northern Italy and as a preliminary to the general withdrawal of the whole Brigade from Greece for this purpose. This withdrawal was perhaps premature because by the end of November the remnants of the Brigade in Athens were in a state of siege in the centre of the city.

The rest of the Brigade with the Independent Platoon were hastily recalled. It sailed from Brindisi and landed at the Pireaus and had to fight its way, with a heavy tank escort provided by the 23rd Armoured Brigade, along the long Pireaus Road into Athens to link up with the remnants of the Brigade in the hotly-assailed vital points.

On 1 December the six EAM Ministers in the caretaker government resigned (no doubt under Communist instructions) and next day a general strike was staged. The remainder of the Cabinet then decreed that all guerilla formations be dissolved. The Communist Party prudently moved its HQ out of Athens, knowing that fireworks must follow. British intentions were again spelled out both by the commander on the spot and by Winston Churchill in a personal statement.

In defiance of government decree, the Communists staged a banned demonstration on 3 December and clashed with the police. The civil war was on. On 4 December General Scobie ordered ELAS to evacuate Athens and the Pireaus. It was a red rag to a bull. ELAS troops and armed civilians tried to seize the capital by force. They succeeded in capturing most of the city's police stations, some with the tacit co-operation of the police, and came within half a mile of the government offices. Three days later war was officially declared on ELAS.

The British Airborne held out in the centre of the city and on 8 December, with the Brigade all back in Athens, General Scobie reported to Winston Churchill: 'Increased activity on the part of the rebels and widespread sniping. Limited progress was made during fighting which continued throughout the day. By midday 35 rebel officers and 524 other ranks of ELAS were captured and are under military guard. Some progress was made by 23 Armoured Brigade in house-to-house clearing throughout the afternoon.

'A further sector in the centre of the city was cleared by the Parachute Brigade. Serious sniping of Navy House, Pireaus by rebels, who infiltrated into the area south of Port Leontos, had to be dealt with by Marines from HMS *Orion*. [*Orion*, it will be remembered, was the cruiser which had taken the Company to Taranto in September 1943.] In face of opposition in one area, our troops were forced to withdraw. In the area being cleared by the Greek Mountain Brigade an attack by the rebels from a flank was held but delayed progress.'

This showed the scale on which fighting was taking place. What the report did not say was that the 5th Scottish spent the whole day forcing their way from Syntagma (Constitution) Square towards the Acropolis and only succeeded in doing so after rushing ELAS HQ in the square itself at the cost of heavy casualties. It was not until nightfall that B Company established themselves on the Acropolis. It was not occupied by the enemy. Today, in normal conditions you can walk from Constitution Square to the Acropolis in 15 minutes.

6th Parachute Battalion had during the day fought their way down the long straight road to Omnias Square. Again a walk of ten minutes at most in normal times. 4th Parachute Battalion held out in the vicinity of the city gas works. Street fighting is never easy. Defenders who know their locality can move from vantage point to vantage point and even double back and appear behind the advancing troops.

In this, the civilians proved an embarrassment. The troops had to provide escort for all kinds of purposes.

One unit had to fetch milk from a single source of supply for the babies. Another had the ludicrous task of rescuing the wife of a Russian diplomat from those whom she thought were her political friends. This sort of fighting went on for a solid hideous week. The Parachute Brigade's casualties mounted to the point where after one month in Greece they exceeded the number sustained in a full six months of front-line service in Italy.

In the Independent Platoon, Lieutenant 'Jock' Boyd (a veteran of the raid on Bruneval) was killed and Sergeant 'Nobby' Yates, one of the old originals of the 21st Independent Parachute Company, along with Private Wolf, won Military Medals for exceptional valour during this fighting which was different from, but comparable with, the ordeal the Company had undergone at Oosterbeek. That the 1st Independent Parachute Platoon played its full part in this week of bloodiness there can be no doubt. Peter Baker refers to the Brigade having to expand its area room by room, house by house and street by street. Every weapon in the Brigade's armoury was employed in the fighting, from PIAT to pistol.

The guerillas had resorted to every low trick and had not hesitated to advance behind a shield of women and children (a tactic later to be encountered in Palestine when dealing with Israeli terrorists intent on escape); four fifths of the guerillas of both sexes and of all ages fought in civilian clothes; they neither asked for nor gave quarter.

A typical incident in the confusion of street fighting is not out of place: snipers active and dangerous operated from housetops; one such post, strongly sandbagged was hard to get at. It was provisioned each day by means of a bucket lowered and raised on the end of a rope. Small children were employed to fill the bucket with the day's provisions knowing the British would not harm them. One morning the post was destroyed by devastating PIAT fire just as the bucket was being lifted over the edge of the sandbags. As the Company had discovered at Arnhem, the PIAT was the most powerful weapon available to the lightly-armed parachutist.

On a visit to Athens on 15 December, General (later Field Marshal Lord) Alexander said:
'If rebel resistance continues at the same intensity as at present I shall have to send further large reinforcements from the Italian front to make sure of clearing the whole Pireaus/Athens area, which is *fifty square miles of houses*.' That gives one some idea of the magnitude of the task.

On 17 December British Intelligence put the ELAS guerillas at 12,000 in Athens and Pireaus. King George of the Hellenes laughed at this and put the figure at between 15,000 and 22,000. The true figure will probably never be known.

At one stage the British, already on half rations, were down to six days' supplies and only three days' reserve of ammunition. The arrival of the 7th British Division in the latter part of December turned the scale. When Winston Churchill arrived at the Pireaus on Christmas Day, to spend the night on HMS *Ajax,* things were fairly well under control and he was able to travel the Pireaus Road into Athens, with an armoured car escort, without incident. He nevertheless recorded that as he was about to go ashore water spouts appeared near *Ajax*. They were caused by shelling from a mile or so to his left on shore.

Meantime, in Britain, sections of the leftist Press were alleging that British troops were being employed to butcher 'innocent workers for the benefit of rich Athenian business men.' The Communist propaganda machine was already at work. The troops, who knew differently, were furious. They had helped to feed the population throughout the battle: had given blood transfusions for the wounded, friend and foe alike, and had borne the brunt of some of the bloodiest fighting in which the Brigade had sustained in one month more casualties than it had in six months' line duty in Italy.

A delegation sent out by the Trade Union Congress under the leadership of Sir Walter Citrine subsequently exonerated the Brigade from these accusations and upheld everything it had done and was doing for Greece. This whole unhappy interlude ended for the Brigade when it was withdrawn from Greece at the beginning of February 1945. Their place was taken by the better part of two divisions.

Back in Italy once more, after a well-earned fortnight's rest, planning began for General Alexander's Spring offensive against the German positions along the River Po. Between 19 March and 8 May (VE Day) more than 30 operations were planned. The Brigade was in a constant state of readiness to support the 8th Army in its offensive. On five occasions the parachutists actually emplaned, but none of the operations took place.

It was a trying time and one which, as all those who served in airborne forces will appreciate, was most testing to morale. Loading aircraft in the heat of an Italian summer in expectation of an operation next day, drawing and fitting parachutes in the same expectation, only to have to return them and unload the aircraft again when the operation was cancelled, was enough to disgruntle the most placid of men.

When VE Day came there was no longer any purpose in keeping the Brigade in Italy. In May 1945 the 1st Independent Parachute Platoon returned to England and was, sadly, disbanded. An association which had lasted in many cases as long as two and a half years, two years of which had been spent overseas, ended. Some few returned to the parent Company and served with it again in Palestine as part of the 6th Airborne Division. Among these was Sergeant 'Jungle' Medlicott. Captain Baker became a Company commander in the 5th (Scottish) Parachute Battalion and also served in Palestine.

Before leaving General Alexander's command Brigadier Pritchard received a letter from the General which said: 'You have a wonderful record of successes and in every battle you have fought you have shown all the true qualities of good soldiers – high morale, dash and fighting efficiency.'

10 NORWAY
V E Day 8 May to September 1945
'The Fruits of Victory'

When most of Europe was celebrating the end of the war in Europe, the Company found itself confined to a camp in the south of England under orders to fly into Norway at the crack of dawn. VE Day (8 May 1945) thus passed uncelebrated so far as the pathfinders were concerned.

Since the return from the Arnhem operation the Company had settled into a routine of barrack life in Newark. It had taken in yet another injection of fresh young blood as it had after the return from Central Mediterranean Forces in 1944. To the veterans of North Africa, Italy and Arnhem the newcomers looked younger than ever. To the eager young recruits the experienced Company they were joining must have appeared a bunch of prematurely old hardbacks. They were soon disillusioned! The men they joined absorbed them as they had the intake before Arnhem, taught them what they knew and found them acceptable. New friendships were formed and the new intake were soon an integral part of the reconstituted Company.

Lt. Col. Wilson DSO, MC continued to preside with Captain R. E. Spivey as his second-in-command. No. 1 Platoon still had Lt. Eastwood MC and Sergeant Binick MM as its commander and platoon sergeant. No. 2 Platoon had Sergeant Allerton MM, but no platoon officer. No. 3 Platoon had its old team of Hugh Ashmore MC and Sergeant Joe Smith MM in charge.

In the period between the return from Arnhem and March 1945 the Company had been without some of its senior NCOs. They had been seconded to the battalions of the 1st and 4th Brigades to help train and build up the many replacements needed in the battalions which had suffered so grievously. Most of these NCOs had no appetite for the task. The war was obviously nearly over and they longed to get back to the Company. There was still just a chance they might be needed again to make some vital landing in Germany itself.

In December 1944 the 6th Division had been thrown into the Ardennes to help deal with the German 'last gasp' counter-attack which had momentarily hit the Americans badly. It had been a bitter winter and the Rhine had still to be crossed.

In the third week of February 1945 the 6th Division had returned to England. Its experience in the Ardennes had added lustre to its history and it was good to see that the pathfinders' sister Company had distinguished itself in the patrol activities of that winter.

When in March 1945 the Company was sent into the wilds of Yorkshire to carry out battle exercises it still seemed possible that the 1st Division might be the one to land in the heart of Germany and finish the war, but on 24 March it was the 6th and not the 1st Airborne Division which dropped east of the Rhine. To some it was a profound relief, to others a source of irritated frustration. The war was as good as over. Those who had seen action were not sorry. Those who had not and had to live with them, longed for something which they could remember and tell their children about! They were not denied their moments of 'glory'. Ahead of them lay landings in Norway and action of a different sort in Palestine.

On the morning of 9 May 1945 two elements of the 21st Independent Parachute Company flew into Norway. It was known that a whole German Army Group existed in Norway, but it was by no means certain that they knew that Germany, through Admiral Doenitz, had capitulated. Nor was it known whether (even if it accepted that the German Army of the West had been defeated) it might still decide to fight rather than surrender.

The platoon sergeants, Binick, Allerton and Smith had all left to undergo the rigours of OCTU. They all achieved commissioned rank. No. 1 Platoon had Sergeant Kent as its platoon sergeant still under Lt. Eastwood. Sergeant Summerville (a veteran, if ever there was one, who had been through Dunkirk, North Africa, Italy and Arnhem) was the new platoon sergeant of No. 3 Platoon under Lt. Ashmore. No. 2 Platoon was without a platoon officer, but it had sergeants like Bill Price, Burns and Wilkin.

The Company was led into Norway by Bob Wilson, who with No. 1 Platoon landed in Stirlings at Gardemoen, near Oslo. The other party was led by Captain Spivey and landed at Stavanger to the west. With him was CSM Stewart and 'Slim' Summerville's platoon.

The reception at Gardemoen was, happily, not hostile. On the contrary, when the handful of Stirlings touched down and taxied into position on the main tarmac in front of the control tower a party of high-ranking German officers, evidently expecting the visitors, emerged and stood at attention as the CO and his escort left the aircraft. Each side formed up and faced each other in correct military formation. Bob Wilson and the Company's other officers, out in front, were treated to a salute from the Germans which they returned punctiliously. After a brief discussion, No. 1 Platoon took over the control tower and its immediate surrounding buildings.

Others were sent elsewhere. Along the road leading to the airfield a whole Panzer Division was lined up. It proved to be non-hostile. The Germans had lost the war and were ready to recognise the fact.

Some of the Company were lucky enough to go, in German transport, into Oslo itself 'to show the flag' and let the Norwegians know that the war was indeed over. The reception they received was of the kind the Company became accustomed to expect wherever it went in liberated Norway. Cheers, kisses, drinks and flowers were showered as vehicles nosed their way through crowded streets.

At Gardemoen there were large numbers of German aircraft parked in orderly ranks around the field, notable Junkers 88s used mainly for North Sea patrols. These were the fighter-bombers which had been used to harass the North Sea convoys on their way to Russia.

One of the incidents which marked the day was the release of Russian prisoners of war from a nearby POW camp. They were a moronic lot. Ill-clad (which they could not help), unkempt and totally undisciplined, they had every appearance of their Mongol and Tartar ancestry. They behaved so badly that by nightfall they had to be locked up again in their old POW camps. Drinking and raping was their way of celebrating their release. Everything was done to get them out of Norway and back on Russian soil just as soon as possible. As Allies they were too much of an embarrassment.

After a day and a night at Gardemoen the Company left in German troop transports, driven by our own men, for Honefoss, a small town about 40 miles north and west of Oslo. Here it settled down to a pleasant existence, making the acquaintance of the locals. After a week or so the rest of the Company, which had landed at Stavanger, joined the Gardemoen contingent. The Company was once more together.

Based there throughout the glorious summer of 1945 the Company was given a number of enjoyable jobs to do. The first of these was a long journey up into the heavily wooded and mountainous country of the Ringerrikke district. The objective was to make contact with the Norwegian Resistance movement and the men who were hiding out to avoid being conscripted to work for the Germans. With the assistance of a couple of Norwegian guides the Company did eventually find the Resistance group, but were left to wonder how, if they ever did, they operated against the Germans in that sort of country, especially in winter.

Back at Honefoss the Company made friends with the local populace and there was not a man who did not 'get his feet under the table' with some Norwegian family. Duties generally were light and there was a lot of time for recreation. Swimming in the river below the Honefoss Falls was popular. So were trips to the fishing lodges around Kingsfjord and out at Rusholm-strana. Parties were frequent and acquaintance was made with the local wartime product called 'acquavite' – a wood alcohol beverage, reputed to turn you blind if overdone!

One of the Company's more dramatic duties was to make sudden dawn raids on the barracks in which the disarmed Germans were confined waiting transport back to Germany. The object of these raids was to single out Gestapo and SS personnel who, on the German collapse, had quietly slipped into Wehrmacht uniform and tried to acquire anonymity in the ranks. With the aid of Norwegians who had so recently been incarcerated in the notorious Grini concentration camp these criminals were identified and handed over to the Military Police to stand trial for war crimes.

The Company's job was to rouse the entire barracks full of

Germans and parade them in long seried ranks on the parade ground just as we found them sleeping in the barrack rooms. It was some small compensation for the discomfort the Germans had caused through the war years now to turn the tables and cause them a little discomfort in return. As the Grini inmates (hooded against being identified themselves) passed along the ranks looking for well-known, well-hated faces, pausing to point an accusing finger every now and then, there must have been many of the Company who thought of friends they had known and lost in action at the hands of these Germans or men like them.

Another task sometimes assigned to the Company was the collection and escorting of whole regiments of Germans from wherever they happened to be garrisoned to the docks at Oslo. One such patrol took No. 1 Platoon to Gol a hundred miles north and west of Honefoss. They were gone three days. At Gol they were punctiliously received by the Camp Commandant, who had his whole garrison paraded ready to march to the waiting train of cattle trucks.

A regimental sergeant major was assigned to Sergeant Kent to order the march. It was all remarkably well-disciplined and the escort provided by the platoon hardly necessary. It provided one of the few opportunities to talk to our old enemies on a man-to-man basis. Mostly, the Germans were very anxious to explain the very real difference between themselves, as members of the Wehrmacht, and the SS and Gestapo, whom they disliked intensely and feared, as long as they still functioned. The nagging doubt that the Wehrmacht and the German people as a whole had allowed and enthusiastically backed Hitler's rise to power and had accepted, as the price of Germany's dominating place in the world, the existence of the SS and Gestapo, could not be entirely dismissed, however. One of the Germans' favourite (and perhaps not entirely naive) themes was that if Britain and Germany could have united in a common cause against Communist Russia, Europe might still be a better place. Looking back over 30 odd years the theory has its attractions. Delivered into the hands of the Military Police at the Oslo docks, the all-conquering Germans who had occupied Norway for the past four years or more, departed unhailed.

For the Company there were more pleasant things to do. Platoon by platoon there was a week's holiday expedition into the Aurdal district where there were fishing cabins to stay in around a large lake. Boats were available for rowing about the lake. Rations were generous. Those who wanted to could swim in the cold waters of the lake. The sun was warm, the atmosphere relaxed. The Company was enjoying its reward for the years of tension now behind them.

There was time to begin thinking of the future. The war was over. The Japs had capitulated on 14 August and although the Company had lost a few of its younger men on draft to the Far East before this happened, the great majority were looking forward to the date of their release. There were those who found it difficult to adapt to this prospect – mostly men who had joined the Army early in the war when they were hardly out of school and were now veterans of four or five years' service. They knew more about Army life and training than they did about any civilian occupation. They were the ones who subsequently made soldiering their career. Others would find their adjustment to civilian life a painful process. They would undoubtedly miss the comradeship they enjoyed in the Company. The longer they had served the harder it would be to make the adjustment.

There were other diversions to come which would fill in the time before the transition to civilian life. Amongst these was a holiday at an hotel at Arendal on the eastern shore of Oslo Fjord. Transport from Honefoss to Oslo, then a train journey of nearly 150 miles of Norwegian coastline took the lucky ones to Arendal. There, they could relax in a hotel overlooking the fjord. By day there was swimming and other sports, good meals and local company. A load of books from England whiled away the hours in sunshine. In the evening, dances were organised and the local girls, suitably chaperoned, made these real social occasions. There were film shows and other entertainment as well. It was as fine a holiday as many had ever enjoyed in their young lives.

This pleasant life could not last. The day came when the Company once more packed its kit, loaded its stores and headed for Oslo and a troopship which carried them back to England via Leith in Scotland. There followed a seven-day leave and a short time in barracks where some of Arnhem's casualties, those who had sufficiently recovered after their release from captivity in May, rejoined the Company. So, too, did some of the men of the old 3 Platoon survivors of the now disbanded 1st Independent Parachute Platoon.

The Norwegian 'holiday' was over. An overseas stint of a different nature lay ahead. Within weeks of return from Norway the Company once more drew tropical kit, reloaded its stores, some of which had not left the crates in which they returned from Norway, did a feverish re-painting of crates and kitbags with new unit numbers and colours for stowing aboard ship, and embarked for the Middle East.

The point of departure this time was Southampton. The destination: Haifa in Palestine.

Norway had been a rewarding experience and at least one of the Company formed a permanent link with that country. Bob Kendall married a girl from Stavanger. By strange coincidence they now live in Ede, so close to the DZs and LZs the Company had marked for Operation 'Market'. Much later, each man of the Company who served in Norway would receive a handsome certificate signed by King Olav commemorating 'The Liberation of Norway 8th May 1945' and reading:

'The people of Norway wish to thank you

....

of the British Armed Forces for your
valuable services in helping to restore
freedom to our land.

OLAV
Oslo, December 1945

A small contingent, which include Peter Holt and Tommy Scullion, had gone back to Arnhem to make a film called *Theirs is the Glory* and rejoined the Company at Newark.

11 PALESTINE
November 1945 to September 1946 – 'The End of The Road'

Early in November 1945 the Company once more passed through the Straits of Gibraltar. In individual cases it was for the third time. It was on its way east to Palestine and it was going there as a direct result of a letter written 28 years earlier by a British Foreign Minister to the then chairman of the British Zionist Federation, Lord Rothschild.

The letter, which was dated 2 November 1917, was written by Arthur James Balfour, a member of Lloyd George's Cabinet and became known as 'The Balfour Declaration'. It included the following passages:

'His Majesty's Government view with favour the establishment in Palestine of a national home for the Jewish people . . . it being clearly understood that nothing shall be done which may prejudice the civil and religious rights of existing non-Jewish communities in Palestine.'

At the time the letter was written, British troops under General (later Viscount) Allenby were still engaged in fighting on Palestinian soil against the Turks, who had been in possession of the country for the preceding 400 years. It is not clear by what right and with what motivation Britain made this, apparently gratuitous 'declaration'.

Although by the end of December 1917 Allenby had defeated the Turks and under the old rules could claim the territory by right of conquest, under the new rules (as formulated by the League of Nations) it did not receive that august body's mandate to govern and administer Palestine until 1920. Nevertheless, the Balfour Declaration gave world Jewry a lever which it used in such a way as to cause Britain acute embarrassment throughout the period of its mandate.

The Jewish return to Palestine was at first slow, but as the flow of immigrants increased, especially after Hitler's persecution of Jews in Germany, Arab hostility mounted until in the years from 1936 to 1939 the British authorities had open revolt on their hands. Then, as later, British troops were called in to assist the otherwise very competent and efficient Palestine Police Force to maintain law and order. Many British soldiers lost their lives there by reason of acts of terrorism on both sides. The Jewish Stern Gang set the pattern for terrorism which many years later would be copied and improved upon by the Palestine Liberation Army operating against the Israelis. The kidnapping, torture and murder of British officers and NCOs and the bombings of well-known buildings became part of daily life in a country where the very existence of the Moslem Arabs, who had been settled there for over 2000 years, was threatened by the influx of a people who during those two thousand years had been scattered all over the world and who now claimed the right not only to return there but to rule the country as an independent state. The British put forward compromise after compromise in the hope of securing peace.

When World War II broke out immigration ceased and an uneasy truce between the Arabs and Jews and the British authorities ensued during the war years. As soon as the war in Europe was over, Jewish refugees released from German concentration camps or able to come out of hiding all over Europe and in parts of Russia, now clamoured to be settled in 'the Promised Land'.

The British resisted the temptation to let the country be flooded with immigrants before adequate means to house and absorb them was available. A quota system was introduced which suited neither Jews nor Arabs. Financed largely from America, Greek and other ships were chartered and illegal immigration started to take place at various points along the Mediterranean coastline extending from Gaza in the south to Nahariva in the north, a distance of rather more than 125 miles.

Assisting in these illegal landings were several Jewish organisations now supplementing the activities of, and to some extent supplanting, the Stern Gang. The Haganah (self-styled 'Self-Defence'), a semi-military body which by the time the

British Mandate ended had a membership of about 50,000, favoured passive resistance. It had no connection with the terrorist activities of the Irgun Zvai Leumi and the Stern Gang. Between them these illegal organisations were set on making British administration all but impossible.

The Palestine Police did its best to cope with the illegal landings and frequent incidents of violence. Arrests were made, ships were intercepted and turned back under escort to Cyprus where camps were set up for the Jews from Europe which they condemned and compared with the treatment they had received at the hands of the Nazis.

British troops, who had just played their part in finishing the war in Europe which led to the liberation of these same Jews, found the Jewish attitude towards them hostile and ungrateful. Small wonder that the troops, sympathy tended toward 'Johnny Arab' who, however unprogressive he might have been in his 2000 years of living in Palestine, was not openly obstructive and seemed to pursue his inoffensive way of life in much the same way as his ancestors had done over the centuries.

It was into this atmosphere of tension that the 6th Airborne Division entered Palestine to assist the Palestine Police in maintaining law and order. The Company landed at Haifa, to commence this thankless task, on 6 November 1945. Immediately after landing it travelled by rail the length of the country to a transit camp near Gaza. It remained there several days until space was found for it more centrally in the long-established barracks at Sarafand. Here it spent a short while and acquired a taste for the gin-based 'Tom Collins' and its variant, the long cooling drink called 'John Collins'.

Soon, however, it was assigned to guard the airfield at Qastina with its complement of Halifax aircraft. Guards of platoon strength had to be mounted each night and jeep and foot patrols around the perimeter took place during the day. Occasional route marches out of Qastina, through Rishon le Zion and to the coast, relieved the monotony of the Company's existence on the airfield. There was no fraternisation with any body of civilians such as had been enjoyed in Norway.

From time to time violent incidents would add a little zest to life and inspire it with some purpose. It was, however, a period of frustration. The enemy operated in civilian clothes and was hardly ever seen. He would strike and then disappear into the civilian background, actively assisted by the local population, women and children alike. The latter were sometimes used as a shield and encouraged to stone British troops called in to form a cordon round a suspect area.

When, after a company-strength guard of the 5th (Scottish) Parachute Battalion was fired on by machine guns from roof tops overlooking the marquee in which they lay resting on Tel Aviv sea front, a search cordon opened fire over the heads of the hordes of obstructing women and children, there was a great outcry about British brutality; entirely exaggerated. No civilians were in fact harmed, but many of the 5th Battalion were killed or wounded by the cowardly machine gunning and others injured by stone-throwing. The provocation offered might well have led to uglier acts of retaliation, but the British troops showed admirable restraint.

A series of explosions in the small hours of the morning on Qastina airfield had the Company standing-to and drawing arms from the armoury where, for security reasons, they were locked away every night. The patrols of the RAF Regiment and the armoured car manned by the Company (on this night by Phil Eden and his crew) had been unable to prevent terrorist infiltration through the perimeter wire. These terrorists had planted a number of 'pencil' bombs and other prepared charges on the undercarriages of some Halifaxes and disappeared into the night before the charges went off. By the time the Company were at full alert the damage had been done and the terrorists easily made their escape.

Road blocks were rushed in all directions, but the whole open countryside could not be covered. In the early hours of the morning, villages and towns in the vicinity were roused and houses searched, but it was hopeless. One civilian looked as innocent (or guilty) as the next and there was nothing to identify the raiders. The crippled Halifaxes lay around the dispersal areas. Too late, it was decided to concentrate them more centrally and to mount a stronger guard in their immediate vicinity.

Shortly before this there had been the notorious planting of explosives in a milk churn, which had destroyed a whole wing of the King David Hotel in Jerusalem, killing and wounding a number of British officers. Yet Jerusalem was one of the local leave centres to which some members of the Company went for a week's rest and change of scenery! In pairs and armed!

Petah Tiqva was another and it was here that Private Cook was shot dead by an over-anxious sentry when returning to camp from a day out. For the first and last time in the

Company's history it staged a military funeral, ably drilled and conducted by CSM Stewart, complete with the slow march of the escorting firing party and six bearers of the flag draped coffin. Our own bugler, Lance Corporal Edgar, sounded the Last Post and the firing party fired its salute over the grave and many thought of those comrades who had departed this life without such ceremony to mark their passing.

On arrival in Palestine, the Company had acquired new platoon officers: Lieutenants Keeling and Walters, fresh from OCTU and Ringway, who came to remain with the Company until it was disbanded. More senior members of the Company began to leave for demobilisation in England. CSM Stewart was one of the early ones along with CQMS McClelland. Their places were taken by Sergeants Kent and Saunders respectively.

From Qastina, one of the last exploits led by Lt. Col. Wilson DSO, MC was a demonstration drop at Amman in Jordania for the benefit of King Hussein. It was an exercise that the two sticks engaged much enjoyed. Soon after this the Company said goodbye to its staunch commander, and Captain Spivey, promoted to Major, inherited command of the Company.

In February 1946 the Company carried out a parachute exercise from Qastina, dropping on soft plough near a 'kibbutz' along the fertile coastal strip south of Rehovat. In March Jews disguised as airborne troops attacked the ammunition dump at Sarafand. In the fire fight which followed a YMCA girl received a burst of Sten gun bullets in the stomach. Thanks to fine surgery she survived.

This was only one of many outrages in 1946. British troops were furious at the weak government policy. Nothing could excuse the lack of determination to maintain law and order. Anti-terrorist activity was considered to be entirely the task of the Police. There was only a minimum of searching and any restrictions placed on the Jews were promptly removed once they objected. The troops spent most of their time on guard. Occasionally they were called out to help maintain cordons and curfews. The Army was locked up behind barbed wire defences or in the Police Forts; their lines of supply, the main roads, were particularly vulnerable.

Nothing could have suited the terrorists better. If the Germans had been as stupid in dealing with European underground warfare there would have been no need for D Day! The Jews had the free run of two-thirds of the country and ran no risk of interference. They could sit and watch the movements of sentries and strike when and where they liked. Sentries grew bored or tired and it was easy to hoodwink them. After an attack, the raiders could disappear amongst their own people in minutes.

There was no danger of running into British troops since all areas designated as 'Jewish' were 'out of bounds' to the Army. Jewish policemen could in no way be trusted to act against their own people and British police were confined to their forts. The policy was 'not to provoke' the Jews. It was a bad policy and one which caused the 'Airborne', an essentially aggressive arm of the Army, much frustration.

Presently the Company made an excursion into the Dead Sea Valley. They arrived at the Police Fort near the bathing and hydropathic resort of Kallia. Nearly 1300 feet below sea level, the Valley was unbearably hot. It was a relief to bathe in the salt water even though it was so thick with saline that it was impossible to sink in it or immerse one's face. On emerging, every part of the body was caked with a fast-drying coat of pure salt. Nor could a 'cold' shower be obtained. The 'cold' water was of bath temperature because of the exposure of the pipes to the heat of the day. After that initial 'dip' on arrival, few went again.

The Company was not there entirely for its health, however. An exercise which took the form of a Company sweep up into the hills to the west occupied a long, hot, dry day. Inter-platoon communications were tested on the old '38' sets and these were supplemented by bugle calls played by the CO's batman, Lance Corporal Edgar. It was on this exercise that some of the Company saw, for the last time, Brigadier Gerald Lathbury.

He pitched up, out of the blue, far out on a hillside not far from Jericho. Sergeant Major Kent would meet him again, 20 years later, at Lake McIlwaine in Rhodesia where, after a Parachute Regiment reunion in Salisbury (Rhodesia) they found a mutual interest in finding and observing the Egyptian pygmy goose and the lesser Jacana or Lily trotter.

During the stay in the Dead Sea Valley, Bill Turner (now in charge of the armoury) and CSM Kent climbed up to pay a visit to the monks living in the remote monastery carved out of the cliff face above Kallia, from which Christ was reputed to have been invited to cast himself by the Devil. A most remarkable place was this, with its own great ornamented bell and tiny paved streets connecting one monk's cell with another. Just what they did apart from pray and meditate was hard to see, but they seemed a remarkably well-fed handful of monks, bearded and simply dressed in long black cassocks with a belly band and small brimless, black fez-like hats. They did not look too clean, but then finding water on those stoney cliffsides must have been a problem.

'Biblical' is the only word to describe the appearance of the countryside. Miles out in the wilderness of this hot and scrubby country a goatherd's plaintive reed whistle could be heard, and here and there the tinkle of bells from the goats themselves. To come upon one of these, usually child-like, goatherds watching his flock from far aloft, was to be cast back into an ageless world far removed from the sophistication of modern warfare: a world which had remained unchanged since before the coming of Christ. There were some who found it preferable to the towns and cities of modern civilisation.

After a few days of this other-worldliness, which suited some more than others, the Company returned to take up its duties in the Police Fort at Latrun. Situated midway between Jerusalem and Tel Aviv, Latrun was a small fertile oasis and a road junction. On one side lay an imposing Benedictine monastery. Here the industrious monks produced excellent wine from the vineyards which they attended in silence. For communication with the public there was a 'duty speaker' appointed daily! We could at least communicate sufficiently to obtain some of their wine.

On the other side, the Latrun prison camp, where many Jewish terrorists were confined, was not such an attractive landmark. On the third side of the triangle sat the square, high-walled Police Fort, with its massive steel doors, commanding, as it lay on a hill top, all the surrounding countryside.

It was built on the same pattern as all Police Forts throughout Palestine around a central courtyard. To be in one was to be any one of the dozens which were dotted at strategic points throughout Palestine. Time hung heavily on the Company's hands at Latrun.

Twenty-four hour guards were mounted, a platoon at a time. A duty platoon stood by each day, ready to dash out and deal with any attempted 'break in' or 'break out' of the heavily wired, top-security prison baking in the sun half a mile away. Early morning drill, PT sessions, weapon training, swimming by platoons (with guards standing by) in a small pool about a mile away and weekly liberty trucks into Jerusalem filled the days.

Gradually, the Company's strength was being depleted as men departed for the United Kingdom via 'the Python Route' for demobilisation. A train down into Egypt across the Suez Canal to the transit camp at Sidi Bishr, thence to Alexandria and a troopship to Toulon in the South of France, a day or two in a transit camp there, then a train across France to Calais and thence to Dover. That was 'the Python Route', travelled by tens of thousands on their way back to civilian life.

Each departure brought to an end close friendships founded on common hardships and experience: friendships which nothing in 'civvie street' could replace. The life of the Pathfinder Company was ebbing to its close. In May 1946 it made another, probably its last, parachute descent in very much the same area as its previous one. It all seemed pointless now. The Company would never function as 'pathfinders' again.

In September, the few remaining officers and men parted company for the last time, posted to various units of the 6th Airborne Division remaining in Palestine. Before the end, however, the Company gained the distinction of having in its rank two boxing champions. Billy Bates won the Divisional welterweight title and Les Nottage the light heavyweight championship. With this flourish the Company disappeared from the British Army's active list, but it would never entirely disappear from the history of Airborne Forces. Nor would it ever cease to exist in the hearts and minds of men who had served with it in its heyday under John Lander, Bob Wilson, Major Spivey and Captain Baker.

In those few momentous, much travelled years, links of a lifetime had been forged. The occasion of its passing was marked by the presentation by Major Spivey, to each of the last serving men of his command, of a cigarette box suitably inscribed with the badge of the Parachute Regiment and the words '21st Independent Parachute Company – June 1942 – September 1946.' Too few of the old originals remained to receive it.

Major Spivey was the longest-serving officer. He had seen it all. From Larkhill to North Africa, from Bizerta to Italy, from Newark to Oosterbeek, to Norway and finally, to Palestine. He had seen men come and go and knew their worth.

As quietly and unpretentiously as the Company had come into existence on Salisbury Plain, so it passed into the shades of military history. Its record of service bears favourable comparison with all that is best in British military tradition. Its memorial is to be found in the Newark Parish Church where a commemorative panel was unveiled by Major General Roy Urquhart. A further plaque is installed in the Church at Oosterbeek alongside the waters of the Lower Rhine.

Author's Note

The following Appendices represent an honest attempt to give credit to all who served with the Company.

They have been compiled to the best of the author's ability from his own knowledge and from the material made available to him.

There may well be omissions. Any omissions are sincerely regretted. They have not been consciously made.

There may be errors in detail. If so, these too are perhaps excusable after the passage of time.

The author invited all ex-members of the Company to make their contribution to this history and he is grateful to those who have responded. He appreciates that the events covered by the history happened many years ago and some matters are best forgotten. Nevertheless, he is quite sure that, remembering the quality and nature of his old comrades, this history would have been the richer had his appeal received a wider response. I am grateful for the correspondence I have received from Peter Baker, Stan Brown, Eric Freeman, Alf Jones, Bill Mollett, Tommy Scullion, Joe Smith, Jim Stewart and Ken Philipson.

These acknowledgements would not be complete without special reference to my friend, Adrian Groeneweg of Oosterbeek, who has shown heart warming interest in the Arnhem operation and the 21st Independent Parachute Company. It was through his efforts that the Company War Diary became available to me. It was his great interest (and kind hospitality when I revisited Oosterbeek in 1976) which was the final spur to my writing this record of the Company's achievements.

RON KENT
3 17th Avenue
Fish Hoek
South Africa.

Appendix A

The following officers and men of and attached to the 21st Independent Parachute Company were killed on active service.

Sicily –1943

Lander Major J. TD.

Italy – 1943

McKnight Private J. – between Foggia and Barletta.

South of France

Morley Private T. ('Terry') – parachute failure.

Oosterbeek – 1944

Avallon Private L. – No. 1 Platoon.
Cameron Private J. – No. 1 Platoon.
Fiely Private J. V. – No. 2 Platoon.
Hillier Private F. ('Umbriago') – No. 3 Platoon.
Horsley Lieutenant J. – Border Regiment attached HQ Platoon.
Jones Corporal J. A. – No. 2 Platoon (probably the first of the Division to die in the Arnhem landings).
Landon Private W. L. – No. 2 Platoon – K.O'd an SP gun and recommended for VC.
Martin Sergeant D. ('Rape') – No. 3 Platoon
May Private M. L. ('Joe') – No. 1 Platoon.
Rodley Corporal J. P. – No. 1 Platoon.
Roberts Private K. ('Darkie')–died trying to swim the river.
Swallow Sergeant Ben C. – died of wounds at Appeldoorn.
Thompson Sergeant E. V. ('Jerry') – No. 3 Platoon.

Greece – 1944

Boyd Lieutenant (Jock) – at Athens.

Palestine – 1946

Cook Private T.

Appendix B

THE KNOWN WOUNDED

It is appreciated that others who were taken prisoner on the banks of the Lower Rhine may have also been wounded before capture.

Italy – 1943

Grierson Lieutenant R. H. – before Apricena.
Sharman Private Alan–whilst trying to escape after Sicily.
Unknown Private (Jewish contingent).
Humphries Private S. see page 66-7.

Oosterbeek – 1944

Alletson Private E. ('Nicky').
Bennett Signalman A. (Royal Corps of Signals attached).
Binnick Sergeant ('Sonny').
Brown Sergeant S ('Stan').
Cadenhead Private G. M.
Cawrey Private V.
Dunbar Private T.
Day Private D.
Eden Corporal P. ('Phil').
Farrow Private K.
Finglass Private G. ('Darky').
Heath Private A.
Hewitt Private D.
Jones Lance Corporal E. G.
Jones Private J.

Lloyd Private A.
McMahon Private T. ('Tommy').
Melford Private I. ('Johnny').
Mitchell Lance Corporal G.
Mitchell Private H.
Moore Private W. ('Barney').
Morris Private J.
Nutter Sergeant E. K., MM (APTC).
Sharlott Private A.
Sharman Corporal Alan (for the second time).
Wilson Major (later Lt. Col.) B. A., MC (later DSO).

Greece – 1944

Wolf Private–MM.

Appendix C

MISSING AFTER OOSTERBEEK 1944
The following is a list of those missing at roll call in Nijmegen on 27 September 1944 whose fate is not recorded elsewhere. Some may have been wounded before capture. All were reported as 'Believed prisoner of war'. Some rejoined the Company after VE Day and served in Norway and Palestine. Some there were who did not return from captivity.

Bence Corporal A.R.
Cockings Sergeant E. G. J.
Bleach Private T. A. (Tim).
Blinko Private G.
Curtis Private G.
Davidson Private -.
Dawson Private A.
Faithorne Private P.
Fletcher Private T.
Ford Private H.
Gentry Private C. R.
Gibson Corporal H.
Gyllenship Lance Corporal W. J.
Hallam Private A.

Hart Private J.
James Private A.
James Private E.
Laing Private A.
Marsland Private S.F.
McEvoy Private A.
Morgan Private T.
O'Brien Corporal T.
Overington Private P.
Pardoe Private A.
Philpott Private A. E.
Reading Private R.
Taylor Private K.
Wilson Private J.
Logan Signalman J. (Royal Corps of Signals).

Appendix D

OFFICERS OF THE COMPANY

Commanding Officers

Lander Major J., TD	founder 1942 – until killed in action over Sicily July 1943.
Wilson Lt. Col B.A., DSO, MC	July 1943 until early 1946 – served with the Company from 1942, slightly wounded at Oosterbeek where he won his DSO and subsequent promotion to Lieutenant Colonel.
Spivey Major R. E.	served with the Company from inception until its disbandment. Succeeded Lt. Col. Wilson as CO in Palestine 1946.

Platoon Officers

Goff Captain	England and Algeria – No. 1 Platoon.
Grierson Lieutenant R. H.	Tunisia and Italy – No. 1 Platoon

	– wounded near Apricena, Italy, 1943.
Baker Lieutenant P.	Tunisia, Italy and later Captain and CO 1st Independent Parachute Platoon, South of France and Greece 1943-1945.
D'Arifat Lieutenant	Tunisia and Italy (from Mauritius) 1943/44.
Ashmore Lieutenant H., MC	England, Arnhem and Norway 1944/45.
Eastwood Lieutenant D., MC	England, Arnhem and Norway 1944/45.
Speller Lieutenant	England and Arnhem 1944.
Druce Lieutenant	England 1944.
Keeling Lieutenant	Palestine 1945/46.
Walters Lieutenant	Palestine 1945/46.

Attached Officers

Campbell Captain ('Jock')	North Africa 1943 – Royal Corps of Signals.
De Beer Lieutenant	South African – Palestine 1945/46.
Horsley Lieutenant J.	Arnhem 1944 – attached as Intelligence Officer from the Border Regiment.
Boyd Lieutenant ('Jock')	5th Battalion attached to 1st Independent Parachute Platoon.
Whiteaway Lieutenant ('Mike')	6th Battalion attached to 1st Independent Parachute Platoon.
Willians Lieutenant ('Dumbo')	4th Battalion attached to 1st Independent Parachute Platoon.

NOMINAL ROLL – OTHER RANKS
AND INDEX

ACTIVE SERVICE CODE

NA – North Africa	A – Arnhem
S – Sicily	N – Norway
I – Italy	P – Palestine
SF – South of France	G – Greece

GENERAL INDEX

PLACES

173

OTHER UNITS AND FORMATIONS – ALLIED

PERSONALIA

BIBLIOGRAPHY

A Bridge Too Far	Cornelius Ryan	(Hamish Hamilton)
Airborne to Battle	Maurice Tugwell	(William Kimber)
Arnhem	Major General R.E. Urquhart	(Cassell)
Bodyguard of Lies	Anthony Cave-Brown	
By Air to Battle	C. Macdonald	(Purnell)
Der Kampf um Kreta	Franz Kurowski	(Gebrüder Efstathiadis)
Hunters from the Sky	Charles Whiting	(Leo Cooper)
Memoirs 1940-1945	Field Marshal Lord Alexander of Tunis	(Cassell)
Memoirs	Montgomery of Alamein	(Collins)
Parachutist	"Pegasus"	(Jarrolds)
The Battle of Arnhem	Christopher Hibbert	(Batsford)
The Fall of Crete	Alan Clark	(Nel Mentor)
The Red Beret	Hilary St. Saunders	(Michael Joseph)
The Second World War	Sir Winston Churchill	(Cassell)
The Struggle for Crete I	McD. G. Stewart	(Oxford)
The Wooden Sword	Lawrence Wright	(Elek)